George Granville Leveson-Gower

Stafford House Letters

George Granville Leveson-Gower

Stafford House Letters

ISBN/EAN: 9783337816568

Printed in Europe, USA, Canada, Australia, Japan

Cover: Foto ©Thomas Meinert / pixelio.de

More available books at **www.hansebooks.com**

STAFFORD HOUSE LETTERS

EDITED BY

LORD RONALD GOWER

WITH TWO PORTRAITS

LONDON

KEGAN PAUL, TRENCH, TRÜBNER & CO., LTD.

1891

PART I.

STAFFORD HOUSE LETTERS.

—•◦•—

INTRODUCTORY NOTICE.

My father was in his twentieth year when these letters to
his mother begin in October, 1806. In the early part of
" My Reminiscences," I have written all that I think can
be of general interest regarding him and his relatives. His
mother, known in later years as the " Duchess Countess "
(of Sutherland), was a person of considerable talent, and
endowed with rare artistic gifts. Her letters—which have
been recently published—to her antiquarian friend and
countryman, Charles Kirkpatrick Sharpe, are full of matter,
and are written in a clear and vigorous style, and display
her love and knowledge of artistic and antiquarian lore.
Her letters to my father, which are at Stafford House with
those now published, mostly relate to private matters,
and are not of general interest. I have therefore, with a
few exceptions, confined this selection of the family letters
at Stafford House to those written by my father to his
mother, togetherwith a few from my mother, also addressed
to the Duchess Countess.

Where there is no note to the contrary, these letters
are all from my father to his mother.

I am indebted to my friend, Mr. J. E. C. Bodley, for
valuable information regarding many of the personages
and public events referred to in these letters.

LETTER I.*

Hamburg, October 24th, 1806.

What bad news † you will hear at the time you receive this ! The Prussians seem to have experienced as complete a defeat as possible. The King of Prussia is gone to Stettin ; he is said to have had two horses killed under him. I will, if I can get it, send you his first manifesto, which is very strong. It is said that nothing can be worse than the conduct of many Prussian officers—bribery and everything bad.

The Duke of Brunswick's life is in great danger, the Prince of Orange and General Mullendorf taken, the French in possession of Berlin. This place is full of people who have fled ; but, as everything is safe here for the present,

* My father, whose earlier letters to his mother are not of sufficient general interest for publication, had, after leaving Oxford, determined to see some of the stirring events that the boundless ambition of Napoleon had forced on Europe. His uncle and future father-in-law, Lord Morpeth, afterwards sixth Earl of Carlisle, had been appointed by the English Government to negotiate with Prussia in regard to the position of Hanover.

In Sir George Jackson's "Diaries and Correspondence" allusion is made to the overtures proposed by Prussia for a renewal of friendly relations with England, which, in consequence of the occupation of Hanover by Prussia, had been broken off. Lord Morpeth embarked on October 1st, at Yarmouth, accompanied by Mr. Bartle Frere, Mr. Ross, and three messengers. He arrived at Hamburg on the 7th. Lord Morpeth's mission was to insist on the immediate evacuation of Hanover by Prussia, and its surrender to Great Britain. The mission was successful. However, the defeat of the Germans caused the total collapse of the Prussians, and Lord Morpeth returned somewhat precipitately to England on October 22nd. My father, as will be seen by his correspondence with his mother, remained with the Prussian head-quarters, where the charm and sorrows of the beautiful Queen of Prussia caused him to linger long.

† This "bad news" was the defeat of the Prussians by Napoleon at Jena and Auerstadt on October 17th, 1806. The court at Berlin had been intriguing with France, and playing fast and loose with England ; but on the settlement of the Confederation of the Rhine, Bonaparte, who had thrown over Prussia, invaded that country and completely routed the Prussian forces. On the date of this letter the Emperor of the French visited the tomb of Frederic the Great at Potsdam, and despoiled it of his sword and the colours which he took in the Seven Years' War, which he sent to Paris to the veterans in the Invalides.

I have determined that I had better stay a day or two, and see how things go on.

And now I will tell a little about myself. On Monday, then, the wind becoming more favourable, at six in the morning we embarked on board Captain Hamilton's packet, and, after experiencing the roughest and most stormy passage that I, the captain, or anybody ever knew, arrived safe at Cuxhaven, last night about six. As it was too stormy then to proceed (though we were very impatient to get here, to hear the news, etc.), we were obliged to remain on board the packet that night; but this morning, at five o'clock, in a Blankansee boat we came up the Elbe to this place, arriving, after a most prosperous voyage, at about three. We went directly to Mr. Thornton's, and to our great surprise learnt that Lord Morpeth left this the day before yesterday; so we must have passed him on the Elbe, as he had made very little way this morning. This annoyed us not a little, but I thought it would be very foolish for me, after such a horrid passage, to return without seeing anything; followed Mr. Thornton's and my own advice, and as the way back is always as much open as at present, I can run no risk by looking a little about me. I have with great difficulty got a room at the "King of England" Inn.

LETTER II.

Hamburg, October 26th, 1806, Sunday evening.

MEINE MUTTER,

Do not read this to my father before you have read *it through.*

I do not feel very confident that I may not be wrong (or, at least, that I shall not get a little scolded) for continuing here, and not taking the opportunity of going back with Lord Morpeth, but if anybody will be so good as to put him or herself in my situation, I must think that, on the whole, they would have acted, or, at least, have been strongly tempted to act, as I have done. In the first place, let me remind and repeat to you what I said in my last letter, which you will have probably received before this, that we really had as unpleasant a passage as I do believe anybody, except Mr. Grenville, ever had, and we have reason to thank God that Heligoland has not been the last that we have been fated to see. We arrived on the evening of the third day at Cuxhaven, as tired and sick as possible, as not having, after the first four hours after we embarked, been able to stand in the vessel ; consequently I arrived at Cuxhaven in the same clothes precisely that I had on at Harwich when we embarked, and I had not been able to eat and drink more than three glasses of negus and one biscuit all the time—I was so sick, or so inclined to be so. We arrived, then, at Cuxhaven as poor as rats, and necessarily, on hearing the bad news when we arrived there, proceeded without delay to Hamburg. On my arrival here I found Mr. Thornton just sitting down to dinner. He asked me to sit down too, just as I was. Now, I could not help doing so, of course, and he sent on the despatches that instant to Lord Morpeth, who had left Hamburg two days before. It was very unlucky that we did not fall in with him on our way from Cuxhaven, but we, you see, came up the Elbe, and he went by land. It was natural enough to suppose that he must by this time have nearly reached Cuxhaven, and certainly natural enough for me to feel very little inclination to set off that moment or evening, or even the next day, to join him, though if I had conceived there was the slightest necessity or prudential reason for my doing so, I should have had no objection.

However, I asked Mr. Thornton what he would do in

my case, and he said, " Stay here by all means," as he would ensure my safety, and that if proceeding towards Russia should be found imprudent, perhaps Copenhagen might be open, and, at all events, the way back to England. Well, now comes what annoys me most. I have this evening received a letter from Lord Morpeth, saying that as he supposed the news I should hear at Hamburg would induce me to return, he should delay sailing a short time for me ; the wind being contrary, must do so too ; and that all accounts were so bad that he would not recommend my proceeding on my journey.

Now says Mr. Thornton, "All accounts he has heard come from me ; I would still advise you to stay," etc. ; and he has been so good as to send with my answer to Lord Morpeth a letter stating his reasons for thinking so. So I still stay; but, moreover, Lord Morpeth sent me a letter which I brought separately from the despatches, in which Lord Howick* says to him, " His Majesty has thought proper to attach Lord Gower to your mission. His lordship is the bearer of this letter, and you will communicate confidentially on all points relating to the negotiation with which you are entrusted." Now, as I had not the least idea of the contents of this letter, and knew that my passport, saying that I was *attaché à la mission du Lord Morpeth*, was only that in cases of difficulty I might get on more easily, I could not suppose, as I fear Lord Morpeth may, that that could be a reason for my returning with him, and as I do not feel that it is so yet, I hope it will not be thought I have, on the

---

* Afterwards second Earl Grey and Prime Minister, 1830-34. His father had been created Earl Grey early in this year, 1806. He thus became Lord Howick, and upon the accession of the Whig administration, also in 1806, he came into office as First Lord of the Admiralty. On the death of Mr. Fox, on September 13th, he became Foreign Secretary, which office he was now holding, Mr. Grenville succeeding him at the Admiralty. His son, the present Earl Grey, still alive in 1890, was already four years old, having been born in 1802.

whole, done very wrong in staying. Things appear so differently to persons in different situations.

I have this evening been with Mr. Thornton to the French Theatre, where there is a pretty good company, and I have been very well amused, and this morning I have been driven about the environs and seen the villas of the Hamburg and Altona merchants, which are all situated on the Danish bank of the Elbe, and some of them are extremely beautiful and have most delightful views of the Elbe. Prince Paul of Wirtemberg is here, a fugitive from the battle. He has quarrelled with his papa, and intended to go over to England; but Mr. Thornton, thinking he would not be particularly useful or acceptable there, advised him not to go, and as he was in the French minister's box to-night, I suppose he has given up the idea.

There are reports here that Bonaparte has been wounded or killed, but have no good foundation, I fear; it is not even known if he was in the battle at all. At the play to-night, in one of the actresses' speeches was some such expression, "Le tyran ne réussira pas toujours." M. de Bousienne looked foolish, and there was a very significantly dead silence.

Sir Brook Boothby came here the same day I did, being driven by the devils. They say that the French had good marksmen who aimed at the officers.

The populace of Berlin are said to be extremely enraged with their ministry, and it is feared they may rise tumultuously, but very little is known here at present. I shall not write more at present, in case to-morrow may produce something.

October 27.—No news to-day. Mr. Thornton is just about to send a messenger, so I shall relieve you from the exertion of reading any more at present from,

Ever yours affectionately,

GOWER.

LETTER III.

LORD MORPETH *to* LADY STAFFORD.*

Devonshire House, November 4th, 1806.

DEAR LADY STAFFORD,

I enclose a letter that I have just received from Lord Gower, as I am sure you must be anxious to hear every account of him.

I have a letter from Mr. Thornton, dated 27th, at Hamburg. He says that Lord Gower continues there at present, and that he is certain of having sufficient notice in case the French approach in that quarter, and that he will take care to give Lord Gower the best advice in his power respecting his route.

The accounts of the Prussian army are rather better than I had reason to expect, but I still entertain no hope.

I have no letters from Castle Howard to-day. I expect to be informed to-morrow of what is determined with regard to Cumberland.

I am under great obligations to the bishop, whatever may be the result.

With regard to Lord Gower, you may consider the retreat into Denmark as perfectly secure.

Believe me very truly yours,
MORPETH.

LETTER IV.

LORD GOWER *to* LORD MORPETH.

Hamburg, Sunday evening, 1806.

MY DEAR LORD MORPETH,

I am exceedingly sorry that I did not write to you by the messenger that was sent off on our arrival the

---

* The Marchioness of Stafford, Countess of Sutherland in her own right, and afterwards first Duchess of Sutherland.

day before yesterday. I had at the time no idea of the contents of the letter I brought from Lord Howick, as the expression in my passport of my being attached to the mission of Lord Morpeth was hardly intended to facilitate my journey. I have consulted Mr. Thornton on the subject of my returning, and he *strongly* advises me to remain here a little longer, as he says he can ensure my safety, and that it may hereafter be possible for me to go *on* to Copenhagen, or somewhere. I am afraid I may be doing wrong in staying, but the temptation is so strong, and it being so excessively provoking to return immediately after a very rough passage, without seeing anything, I am induced to remain. If I am the cause of your being delayed a moment for me, I shall be inconsolable, and if you do not pardon what must seem such an extreme inattention on my part, as not having written to you before, and which I am astonished did not appear to me so at the time as much as does at present.

Believe me, my dear Lord Morpeth,

Very affectionately and sincerely yours,

GOWER.

On receiving your letter I had ordered a chaise immediately, but Mr. Thornton having given me leave to say that he strongly advises my staying, I have availed myself of his permission.

LETTER V.

Hamburg, October 30th, 1806.

As it does not seem quite convenient, etc., to pursue one's journey through Germany at the present moment, I shall follow the plan which we thought of at Trentham, namely, of going to Copenhagen ; and when one tires of that, to Stockholm, etc., is a very easy and practicable journey. No news to-day of importance. The Duke of Brunswick arrived yesterday evening at Altona. Bonaparte vows vengeance against him, and says he will catch him wherever he can, and that none of his race shall ever have any authority, etc., as long as he can prevent them.

The cruelties of the French, they say, exceed everything.

Six houses at Weimar burnt to the ground, and all plundered dreadfully, because some French officer was shot at by a student.

Bonaparte intended to be at Berlin on the 25th. I will now tell you something very confidentially, which is, that the Hamburgers think that Lord Morpeth has been in this too hasty in his return, and that he ought to have stayed here a little to see how affairs went on, in case there might have been a possibility of his joining the King of Prussia. Though I do not think that has hitherto been the case, yet they say it might have been. However, they may be wrong, and Lord Morpeth, I suppose, consulted Mr. Frere and Marsh, and they are, besides, not quite pleased with the joy they showed at having escaped ; for, as they were very nearly the first people that brought the bad news, the pleasure they felt, very naturally, at having so narrowly escaped seemed rather ill-timed to the people here, who had no particular reason for rejoicing at anything that had happened, and were almost all extremely dejected at the melancholy turn of things in general. Now, I would not have you tell any one person in the world, except a *little boy*,* that I have said this, so you had better burn the letter, and not remember that you have heard it—at least, from me.

* My father here probably alludes to his brother, Francis Gower—afterwards Earl of Ellesmere—born in 1800.

I must own that this was also my private opinion, even
before I heard that it was the general one here.   There
were even little printed cards circulated here in ridicule of
his sudden departure.   If you tell anybody that I have
said this, I will never write confidentially to you again.   I
have paid for two copies of the map of Westphalia, part of
which has come out; I have ordered them to be directed
to the Marquis of Stafford, who will be so good as to send
one to the Dean of Christ Church, as I promised him one.
The Duke of Gloucester * has been so good as to send me
a letter for the Duchess of Brunswick ; I shall write to
thank him, though it is not likely to be useful as things
are.

I shall set off for Copenhagen with a messenger the day
after to-morrow.   I go to the French play every evening,
which is always so much gained.   Sir J. Sinclair's son is
at Gotha ; † his situation, I should think, is unpleasant.   I
have bought a little watch (like Puysegur) for Char.,‡ to
console her.   Lord J. Fitzroy will convey it to England,
though it is hardly worth sending, as, I suppose, such can
be got in London; however, this comes from Geneva.
Bonaparte said to the Duke of Brunswick's messenger,
" Dieu dispose des cœurs, moi je dispose des hommes ; le
Duc de Brunswick a cessé de regner."

They say the road to Copenhagen is very good.   You
will write to me there.

Ever yours affectionately,

GOWER.

* William Frederick, second Duke of Gloucester and Edinburgh, had just
succeeded his father, the brother of George III.   In 1816 he married his
cousin, Princess Mary, the king's daughter, but died *s.p.*   His mother was
the Countess Waldegrave, a natural daughter of Sir Edward Walpole, son of
Sir Robert, and brother of Horace Walpole.

† Gotha was invested by the French.

‡ The sister of the writer, Lady Charlotte Gower, afterwards Duchess of
Norfolk.

LETTER VI.

Hamburg, November 1st, 1806.

I take the opportunity of Lord John Fitzroy, who is on the point of setting off this morning for London, of sending one copy of the map as far as it goes, the bookseller here not having any more yet. I shall set off this evening with the messenger to Copenhagen, for as it is not impossible that the French may come here, though Mr. Thornton does not think they will, yet it is as well not to wait till we hear they are on the road, as the bustle and confusion here would make it difficult to get horses, etc.

I yesterday bought a very tolerable carriage for twenty-five guineas.

If you know anybody at Copenhagen, or anybody that knows anybody there worth being recommended to, recommend me.

P. Bariatniskie has given me some letters. I have not heard any news this morning, and as I wrote to you the day before yesterday, you shall not have any more at present from,

Ever yours affectionately,

GOWER.

LETTER VII.

Copenhagen, November 8th, 1806.

I announced my arrival at this metropolis two days ago, and am quite sure that you all think I have done well in coming here; and if you do not, let me assure you that I think it is the truth. Mr. Garlike is very civil to me, and asked me yesterday to dinner to meet some of the principal merchants here, and afterwards he paid a great many visits with me to the principal noblesse, etc., who are on the whole no very great things. I am to dine with him again to-morrow, with some of the corps diplomatique, etc.

I think I shall leave this place in the beginning or middle of next week, and shall be presented to the King of Sweden, and then go to Stockholm, where two days will, I believe, be sufficient to see everything worth seeing (here I am interrupted by an invitation from the Chevalier de Lizakivitz to dine with him on Tuesday. He was the Russian Minister in England for a great many years, and is very fond of England, and is their ministre plénipotentiaire here at present, and very popular, and gives great dinners), and I shall receive some letters from you at Petersburg.

The Danes are all very sorry at the French success, but they pretend to be under no alarm for themselves, as they say they have always acted with so much prudence. I do not feel much annoyed at talking French; it is wonderful how well some of the Danes talk English. I told you in my last letter that I was not particularly delighted with what I had seen of the country, but they say that I have only seen the worst part of it. You may believe them as you please. I like Roth very much; he is very attentive and active.

People dine here at four, and have dinner brought up dish by dish, and pay visits in the evening. We were fortunate enough to find everybody at home last night, generally drinking tea and playing at cards; but Mr. Garlike says they are not very gay, and live very quietly and dully in general.

There is only a Danish play. No news to-day, as it is none that I am

Very affectionately yours,

GOWER.

LETTER VIII.

Copenhagen, November 15th, 1806.

Mr. Garlike received an order yesterday to have a frigate ready to secure a Colonel Sontag employed in our service passage to Pillau, to enable him to meet the King of Prussia, wherever he may be, so that on my landing with him, if it be not safe to go to the King of Prussia, I shall at all events be so far on the Russian road ; this is the last letter you will receive from this place, where I have stayed two or three days more than I at first intended, to give the King of Sweden time to come to Malmo, that I might see him on my way to Stockholm. For the good reasons which follow, I have given up that plan, and he will not have the honour of seeing me (this year at least), as I shall take the opportunity of a frigate going up the Baltic, which will be infinitely preferable. Char.'s experiments have hitherto failed, but she must not despair yet. I am almost ashamed to say that I do not regret that I stay for so short a time here, for I have every reason to thank the inhabitants for their civilities, as I have dined out every day, one day at Comte de Schimmelman, premier ministre, and the others with ministers, merchants, and gentlemen ; and the dinners would be more agreeable if they were of less duration. They are not by any means splendid.

The poor Duke of Brunswick is dead. Holstein is full of princes and princesses, some of whom are coming here, and some you may have, for in Holstein they are not very safe. A great part of the ministry, etc., here are better inclined to the French than they should be. God help them if Bonaparte comes here, which I should think not impossible ; but it is better to hope that the Austrians will come up, and something be done yet, when he has advanced a little further. The accounts to-day state that Magdeberg is taken.

I see in the papers which Mr. Garlike has just sent me that Lady Alva,* as might be expected, is no more. How enviable her end is, compared to the poor Duke of Brunswick's, whom one cannot help pitying! The French have had a little affair with the Danes, in spite of neutrality ; but they have only killed twenty-one men, and then say it was a mistake, which the poor Danes must swallow, and when the French ask for their fleet, they must give it.

I expect my *compagnon de voyage* every minute. I suppose we shall set off the moment he comes.

I like Mr. Garlike very much ; he sometimes looks very melancholy.

I dreamt last night that Lord Granville was married. I have thought fit to tell you so, in case it should be true, to confirm your faith in dreams. I hope my father and Char., etc., are well. I shall hear when I arrive at Petersburg.

Ever yours affectionately,
GOWER.

A Danish general, who went to the French general to complain, was treated very civilly, and sent back with an escort, who took his watch and purse from him by force.

LETTER IX.

Elsinore, November 24th, 1806.

We have been kept here by contrary winds since Tuesday, but now have hopes of sailing to-morrow morn-

* Lady Alva was my father's maternal great-grandmother.

ing for Königsberg, where it is thought the King of Prussia is, and at all events the queen. I am vexed not to have seen the King of Sweden, but I could not have gone to Malmo, where he is, and returned in less than three days, and the risk of the wind having changed in that time was too great.

I was very glad indeed to receive a letter from you just before I left Copenhagen, as I was made certain by it of your approving of my plans so far, but I have not received the letter in which you mentioned Lady Alva's death.

My *compagnon de voyage*, Colonel Sontag, has the reddest, loudest, longest nose I ever saw. I shall take the first opportunity of announcing its safe arrival at Königsberg, and though the season is rather late for voyages, if the weather is as fine with you as it is here, you can be under no alarms. Mr. Garlike has given me a letter of introduction to C. Haugwitz. I wrote to Granville to desire him to write one to Mr. Stuart for me two days before I received it with yours at Copenhagen.

Pray do not be disappointed when you see me come home without any Danish drawings, for I have travelled *too quick* through the country; have seen nothing tempting, and it is the month of November.

However, as the weather will be warm before I come home, and I shall have seen a good variety by that time, perhaps I may try. Did I tell you that when in town I mentioned Murray to Mr. Grenville, but he did not seem to think it likely for him to have any opportunity to do him any good, at least in his present situation?

This place has nothing worthy of mention. The Princess Royal has a small house and garden near it, all very small and much neglected; the situation of the gardens something like Dunrobin.

C

The passage of the Sound is about the same as the Muckle Ferry. I marvel at Rugantino. What is become of Sir J. Wrottesley?* I shall not send this till we are *actually* setting off.

The Princess of Weimar (Grand Duchess of Russia) is in Holstein, and will probably set sail in an English ship for Lisbon, as the Emperor of Russia has sent to beg her to come.

You have heard that the French have entered Hamburg.†

Ever yours affectionately,
GOWER.

LETTER X.

Dantzig, December 2nd, 1806.

This is the seventh day since we embarked at Elsinore, and after tossing about six days we arrived here yesterday evening, and have this moment disembarked.

As the king and court are at Königsberg, I shall proceed thither without loss of time. I have not yet had time to hear any particulars as to news; there is a report, however, of the Russians having beat the French at Warsaw.‡ The Prussians are assembling all the men they can get together about Königsberg, and there is a very strong garrison (six regiments) here.

* Afterwards raised to the peerage as Lord Wrottesley.

† The French, under Mortier, entered Hamburg on November 19th. The British merchants were placed under arrest, and the magazines of corn conveyed to Berlin, where Bonaparte was. On November 20th he promulgated his decree, declaring the British Islands in a state of blockade, and prohibiting all commerce in English produce and manufactures.

‡ This news was premature; the French, however, before the end of the month received in Poland their first serious check on the Continent, when they were routed at Pultusk (see p. 24).

As the post is, of course, entirely broke up, I do not know how soon you will have any chance of hearing from me again. I shall send this letter by the captain of the sloop, the *Ruilleur*, who brought us ; if we had had a fair wind all the way we should have been here in forty-eight hours, but it was contrary till the last day, and two of the nights were terribly *squally*.

I am very glad to be on *terra firma* again ; the ground is covered with snow,. and the weather very cold. I have not been *sick*, but obliged to stay in my cot almost all the time. My voyage has put me a good deal in mind of our Scottish one, and the first lieutenant is a Peterhead man, and says, "Deed is it ! "

It will be an odd sort of sight to see the Prussian court in their present state, won't it ? Remember to write to Petersburg, and make Char. too.

Of course, I do not yet know how soon I shall get there, as that must depend on circumstances.

We have just seen the Governor, General Manstein, who says the king is determined to hold out to the last.

Yours ever affectionately,

GOWER.

LETTER XI.

Prussian head-quarters, Wehlau, December 8th, 1806.

Look at a narrow neck of land running from Dantzig to Pillau ; along that we travelled, and arrived at Königsberg, which is a very extensive town, on the 5th.

The 6th we spent in paying visits to Count Schulenburg, Baron Hardenberg, General Kalkreuth, and the Princess of Solms, sister to the queen, who is a very agreeable person. Yesterday we arrived here, and called on the minister *pro tempore*, the Councillor Beyhm (Haug-witz being dismissed), and last night came an invitation from the king to dine with him to-day. At Ortelsburg, the last head-quarters, the queen had only one small room to eat and sleep in, and that full of bugs, etc.

They are better off here, but I believe the lodgings I am in are almost the best in the place. They were destined for the English Legation, but as there is no such thing, they have given them to me. People have, I fear, here been a little disappointed with me, as they all seem to have expected to see a plenipotentiary ambassador. The Princess of Solms said she expected the queen at Königsberg in a day or two, but that she supposed my arrival would keep her here a little longer; and she was quite surprised that I was only a *voyageur en particulier*.

It is a great pity we have no minister here. Young Jackson, our Prussian minister's brother, has been with them for some time, but he is only a *particulier* also.

General Buxhoven's army of Russians is to join General Benigsen's * on the 10th, so we may soon expect a blow to be struck, and it will be a fine thing to be so near if any victory takes place. 'If not, I can easily remove myself. At all events, the road I have taken is a more interesting one than through Sweden, and I think on the whole, so far, I have been extremely fortunate. I shall not write any more till after the king's dinner, when I may perhaps hear some news.

Well, I am just returned from the dinner, which has been very agreeable; and after it I had a long talk with the queen (who is a very charming person), that Bonaparte is the devil, and that he cannot hate her more than she him. Colonel Sontag is going to the Russian head-

---

* Chief in command of the Russian forces in Poland, who commanded at Pultusk and Eylau, described in letter xix.

quarters, and will take this for me to Sir Hertford Jones, who is going to England and will take this.

You may tell Lord Harrowby, Lord Granville, and Mr. T. Grenville that the queen talked of them, and that Baron Hardenberg, who is now "out of office," desired to be remembered to the two former.

I must conclude for the present, and you cannot wish for a better conclusion than that I am very well, in good spirits, and better amused than at Oxford.

Ever yours affectionately,
GOWER.

LETTER XII.

Königsberg, December 11th, 1806.

I am sure you can have no reason to complain of not receiving plenty of letters from me. I sent one two days ago from Wehlau, the Prussian head-quarters, by a Sir Hertford Jones, late consul at Bagdad, in which I told you of the royal dinner. The king and queen came yesterday here, and almost everybody else among whom I am to-day; they say that the king will go back to-morrow, but I do not believe it, especially as the account came yesterday of General Victor's having passed the Vistula at Thurm, taking advantage of some neglect of General Lestock. The Russian general, some days ago, wanted a prisoner or two, from whom he might obtain some information, on which a party of Cossacks swam over the Vistula, attacked a party of French, killed all the private men, and made two officers swim back with them, dragging them through the river by the hair. Mr. Wynne and a little Mr. Walpole arrived late last night at Wehlau from Vienna, and bring *no* account of the Austrians coming forward as we could wish here. I

condole with you on your being blockaded by Bonaparte.*
I have just received an invitation to dinner to-morrow
from General Kalkreuth, when we shall probably hear
some complaints of the ill-usage he thinks he has met
with from the king, and abuse against Prince Hohenlohe
and others. This letter will go by the last merchant ship
from this place, but I dare say I shall find means to let you
hear from me again soon. Give my love to my father,
Char., etc., etc.

Ever yours affectionately,

GOWER.

If you hear any accounts of a considerable Prussian
army being still in existence, do not believe them. Their
remains are very inconsiderable.

LETTER XIII.

Königsberg, December 15th, 1806.

I really and truly do believe that I have hardly lost one
single opportunity, since the beginning of my travels, of
letting you know that I am flourishing, and not in the
hands of the French.

Mr. Burrel, who has come with Mr. Wynne from Vienna,
is to sail as soon as he can for England, and of course I
cannot allow him to go without a letter from me, though
I have nothing to say worth sending. The people of note
that I have seen since I wrote two days ago are Prince
William and Princess Louise, sister to the unfortunate
Prince Louis,† who was killed at the beginning of the war.
She seems to be an agreeable person enough, though at

* See note on p. 18.
† Prince Louis of Prussia was killed at the Bridge of Saalfeld about a week
before Jena.

first the conversation was not very amusing ; for, as Wynne was acquainted with Prince Louis, she talked of him a good deal, crying much for some time.

The queen has been very ill, confined to her bed, ever since she arrived here, and so, indeed, have a great many other persons, with the " cholick," which, I suppose, will, in addition to other reasons, induce the king to remain here, where I think he would have done well to have come some time ago, instead of moving from one little village to another.

There is nothing like news to-day, though we think we must hear something soon. Lucchesini has been sent off from Berlin, and is expected here.

It is not known yet who is to be minister ; Stern has refused more than once, and it is hoped that the king will be obliged to appoint Hardenberg. Such mild weather for December was hardly ever known. We have heard nothing from England since about the 11th of last month. I am surprised at Rugantino, and am

Ever affectionately yours,

GOWER.

Wynne stays with the intention of acting as minister here—at least, till our Government appoint somebody.

LETTER XIV.

Königsberg, December 23rd, 1806.

A week ago I made preparations for leaving this, and setting off for St. Petersburg ; but the day before that I had fixed on for departure I received a letter from Lord Hutchinson, saying that he had arrived at Dantzig with much the same powers and instructions as Lord Morpeth had, and that Mr. Garlike had informed him of my having left England with the intention of joining Lord Morpeth, etc., and that he hoped that I should find no change in my condition from the alterations; than all which, you see, nothing could be more civil. I have, in consequence, stayed to see Lord Hutchinson,* who arrived here yesterday, and has been so kind as to show me his instructions, and to be extremely civil, so I think the best thing to do will be to remain with him some time longer, and see how things go on. I have no news to tell. Bonaparte I believe to be still at Posen. The French, who had crossed the Vistula and advanced to Graudenz, are said to have retired. Lord Hutchinson had a very narrow escape in the *Astrea* frigate, in the Cattegut, having struck on the Anhalt reef; they were obliged to throw the guns overboard, and cut down the masts. He came from Copenhagen in a sloop ; he will probably go to the Russian head-quarters. I am sure Lord Morpeth must have repented of his return. The weather is mild, but they say the dysentery prevails among the French.

LETTER XV.

Königsberg, January 1st, 1807.

A happy New Year, and many returns, etc. I was very happy to hear from you the day before yesterday, when I received the Baron de Rolls' letter. Lord Hutchinson, etc., have arrived and are still here, with what there is of the Prussian court, but whether we shall all decamp suddenly or stay on depends on whatever news we may at any moment hear. Reports spread by the dozen. Yesterday morning came a courier announcing a victory gained over the French

---

* Father to the first Earl of Donoughmore, and the successor to Sir Ralph Abercromby in the command of the army in Egypt.

by the Russians, under Benixon,* near Pultusk, but this proves, I fear, to be a very useless victory, as well as another by Buxhoven, as the Russians are said to be obliged to retreat, and that the commander-in-chief, Kamenskoy (?), has run away in his shirt, like a mad fool.

I am prepared to set off at five minutes' notice, as I have bought some horses for that purpose. If we are obliged to run off, we shall all go to Memel.

I like Sir C. Wilson very much indeed ; he will probably go to the Russian army, if it keeps its ground. Lord Hutchinson says that he could not have conceived such a thing as the Prussian ministry, but that the king has more sense than he imagined. The queen is still very ill, con-fined to her bed, but rather better ; it will be shocking, if the French come here now, for her to travel in such weather, but if frost sets in, we shall get on prosperously. Wynne will take this to you ; he is to set off this evening.

I am very glad to be here, so near everything. Bona-parte is said to be on this side the Vistula in his own person, but nobody knows anything *for certain.* Zastrow is minister, Schulenburg and Hardenberg out entirely, and Haugwitz. I have written a great many letters to you, as I suppose nearly half may never arrive at the place of their destination.. Give my love to my father, Char., etc.

Ever yours affectionately,
GOWER.

You may tell anybody you see that they may write to me to Petersburg.

* This is the Russian general whose name is spelt Benigsen in letter xi., and Bennigsen in letters xvi. and xvii.

LETTER XVI.

Memel, January 9th, 1807.

In spite of the two victories of the Russians over the French (which, in fact, were only trifling affairs between the advanced posts), *nous voici*, of all roads in this world, that from Königsberg by the Strand to Memel is the worst. I came with Lord Hutchinson, etc., with our own horses, and our carriages were every moment buried so deep in the sands and snow, that we were obliged to get out of them and help to extricate them, and this journey, short as it is, lasted five days.

We arrived the day before yesterday; the king, etc., yesterday. The queen is said to be rather better for her journey; she to-day walked a little in her room for the first time. She is almost the only person one is really sorry for of the Prussians.*

The French are said not to have entered Königsberg yet, but they probably will not remain long out of it, as there is nothing to hinder them from taking it at any time; and if the frost is really set in, of which there is every appearance, they will soon cross the Memel river, and drive us from hence, unless the king makes a separate peace.

The Russian officers have held a council of war, in which they have declared their general, Kamenskoy, a madman. Bonaparte's good fortune is certainly most wonderful, in having opposed to him a man who one day, in his shirt, decorated with all his orders, runs about to encourage his soldiers, and the next stripped himself naked to show his wounds to his surgeon, and obtain a certificate from him, and then leaves his army.

* There was a strong feeling in England that Prussia had only got her deserts for her intriguing with Bonaparte and her treachery to her British allies.

Lord Hutchinson is very kind to me, and shows me his despatches, all which induces me to stay here a little longer to see the end of all this before I set off for Petersburg.

Ever yours affectionately,

GOWER.

They declare here that it is not true that the French have the sword of Frederic, as they have brought it away, and I am to see it. My last letter went from Königsberg by Wynne.

January 17th.

I have hardly anything to add, except that Buxhoven, who was next in command to Kamenskoy, has received his dismission, and that Bennigsen has the command. Murat is very ill at Warsaw. Nothing of consequence has happened lately. The queen is much better. Give my love to all proper persons.

LETTER XVII.

Memel, February 7th, 1807.

We are in almost hourly expectation of hearing the account of a decisive affair having taken place between the Russians and French, and are in extreme anxiety lest the event should prove unfavourable. Bennigsen, with twenty thousand, was on the 4th near Gutstadt, intending to retreat to Allenberg, his object being to avoid a grand battle, and the French were close upon him, having got between him and General Essen, who, with they say about forty thousand, is at is not known where.

The Russians are in excellent order and high spirit, but Bonaparte's generalship, it is to be feared, is superior to Bennigsen's. Some days ago, at Monungen, the Russians had an affair of advanced posts, and took Bernadotte's baggage, but no material advantage has hitherto been gained on either side; but one dreads the account which the next message may bring. I shall keep my letter open till the last moment that the ship which is to take it will allow; for, if the wind be fair, she will sail to-morrow. I shall tell the captain to take this to you, and a parcel with it, in his own person; so tell Lilly to ask him to dinner in the steward's room.

The parcel contains a gown of the Queen of Prussia. She has given it to me to have a morning dress made in London, of the same size, and, I believe, the same sort of stuff, but that I leave to your taste. She begs that it may not be very expensive; and you must find a watch that repeats the hours of its own accord, which she intends to give to the *grande maitresse*, the Countess de Voss, a very good old lady, who does not care if the watch is old fashioned or new, but it must go well.* Now, God only knows where the queen may be obliged to fly to at the time you receive this, so that it is impossible for me to tell you how or where to send the gown, etc., but you must consult those who are most likely to know the surest way of sending it to her, wherever she may be. I wish you were acquainted with her; you would like her so very much, and she is so much to be pitied. You can have no idea what an amiable, charming person she is. She is hardly recovered yet from the fever, which has been very dangerous.

If they are ever re-established (but Bonaparte said lately that he should appoint a new king), you must go to Berlin to see her. The gown I would advise you to keep

* The Countess de Voss, whose life and diary have been published, was *grande maitresse* to the Queen of Prussia. She was born in 1729, and was brought up at the court of Sophia Dorothea, daughter of George I. and wife of Frederick William III. of Prussia.

as a souvenir, though the doing so may not be quite honest ; but you can have two made instead of one, and I will hint to her the possibility of its not returning in proper person to her, so do not mind my father if he insists on its being sent back.

LETTER XVIII.

February 8th, four o'clock.

Just come from dinner at the king's, who is, as you may suppose, rather low-spirited.   However, to-night we are all to drink tea at Princess William's—king and queen, etc. Bennigsen has reached Wehlau.   His situation is disagreeable.   I am sorry that I must send this off before something is heard, but the ship is ready to sail and cannot wait.

Believe me, ever yours affectionately,

GOWER.

I see in the paper that A. H. Jones has dined with you. A messenger arrived from England yesterday, the first that Lord Hutchinson has received since his departure.   Mr. Hutchinson and Sir R. Wilson are with the army.   Give my love to everybody, and tell Char. to write.   Adieu.

LETTER XIX.

From MR. HUTCHINSON *to his brother,* LORD HUTCHINSON, *after the Battle of Preussisch Eylau.*

Königsberg, Monday, February 9th, 1807.

The different marches of the Russian army from Monungen, which we left on the 3rd instant, to Preussisch

Eylau, where we arrived on the 7th, having taken the direction of Jankova, Wolsdorf, Frauendorff, and Landsberg, you are already acquainted with. The first movement to Jankova, in the neighbourhood of Allenstein, which the enemy had approached, you cannot but have censured, the more so as General Bennigsen had declared that it was his object to avoid a general action, at the same moment placing himself in a situation where it was evident he must fight, should the enemy wish it, or dispirit and weary his troops by night marches and over leagues of land, in order to avoid, as long as possible, the evil moment which was to decide the fate and interest of all the powers of Europe. On the 4th the enemy failed in his attempt to dislodge us from two different parts of our very extended position at Jankova, but on the evening of that day he pushed forward a corps, and made rather an obstinate reconnoissance. The defence of the rear-guard of the Russian army during the four following days against a much superior force was vigorous and able.

On the evening of the 6th, at Landsberg, the enemy, having driven in the rear-guard, showed himself for the first time in force on the opposite hills to our camp, when night prevented his attempting anything. On the following evening, at Preussisch Eylau, he took possession of that village, which lay at the front of our position in a valley, separating us from a range of sand-hills, over which he had to pass in approaching from Landsberg. We had taken up our position on the morning of the 7th, and had originally occupied this village and two others in the same valley towards our right, but all of which were, on the approach of evening, abandoned by our troops, owing to some mistake.

The enemy, who had advanced a corps along the range of hills in our front, immediately pushed for these villages,

particularly for that of Preussisch Eylau, from which he was
at length driven with considerable loss on both sides, but of
which he again took possession during the night ; this village
having been a second time abandoned by the Russians,
though not attacked—I believe owing to the general who
commanded there being wounded, and who had retired
behind the camp to the head-quarters to be dressed, having,
however, left another general to fill his place. The position
of the Russians, from right to left, extended about one
English mile, and from front to rear nearly as much. To
the right the country was open for a considerable way, but
on the *left*, at some little distance, were woods and ravines.
The front was strong, in consequence of the valley I have
mentioned, and from the nature of the hills opposite, from
which the enemy had to descend, he could not approach
with an extended front ; besides, in his ascent from the
valley to the Russian position, he had to encounter a very
formidable range of batteries, consisting on the whole, along
the front line, of nearly one hundred pieces. The whole of
the Russian and Prussian artillery amounted (as they inform
us) to seven hundred pieces ! Several guns were placed
during the night at that point of our position which over-
looked the town of Preussisch Eylau, and at daybreak yesterday morning this battery was opened against the town.
After a little time a strong column of infantry issued from
the town and advanced near to this battery, from which
they were driven with considerable loss, when they fell back
on a strong corps of troops, posted at some distance opposite, in one of the ravines which ran nearly parallel to our
front, therefore not commanded by it, and consequently
could not be enfiladed by our cannon. At the same time
the enemy appeared in several lines on the opposite hills,
further back than this, first extending along our front and
particularly annoyed us from the villages by their tirail-

leurs. They had brought up also, in different points, some guns, which, however, had little effect, whilst our batteries were making a most tremendous noise to as little purpose. After some time the enemy annoyed us much by the fire from several heavy pieces of ordnance, which he had most judiciously and with great quickness placed on the commanding points of the opposite hills ; and at length, availing himself of the smoke and a snowstorm, he attempted to reach our first line with two strong columns of infantry, which were literally cut to pieces by the Russian cavalry, notwithstanding the ocean of snow through which they had to wade, and that downhill. The enemy again had recourse to his batteries, from which we suffered much, when at last his cavalry had the boldness to advance, and did actually reach our lines, when it suffered much, and from whence it was in a very short time driven by our cavalry, whose conduct then, during the whole of the day, and in all the affairs of rear-guards, has been most heroic. The sharp-shooting and discharge from the batteries still continued to do us some mischief, but by the hour of twelve —that is, about five hours and a half from the commencement of the action—the advantages were all on the side of the Russians, who had certainly lost many men by the intrepidity, perhaps inconsiderate rashness, of their cavalry in charging through ground where they were exposed to great disadvantage, but where, notwithstanding, they were always successful, and gloriously so. Still I say, notwithstanding their losses from this and other attacks from batteries, etc., all the advantages were to the Russians, and hitherto the enemy had completely failed. He had, I suppose, very early experienced how impossible it was to attack us with success in front.

On our right the country was open for a considerable distance, so that we could have been apprised immediately of any advance from that quarter; not so the left, where, as I have informed you, there were sand-hills and wood.

There had been repeated requests made to the Russian chiefs to be most active in watching the enemy's movements in this direction, and I was assured that every necessary precaution had been observed. The distance from the extreme left to where the attacks in front were made did not admit of personal observation. At about one o'clock, however, notwithstanding our success, some of the Russian corps of infantry fell back from the left, where at the moment they were not attacked, as also some corps of cavalry, though covered with glory. At this instant the enemy (who had been, I doubt not, for some hours getting his troops through the different defiles and woods on our left) appeared in the rear of the left, where he had already succeeded in bringing up, with certainly vast difficulty, some pieces of artillery, which he placed on the summit of the ridges, and from whence he succeeded, by his fire, to convert the heroes of the morning into the very cowards of the evening ; for neither cavalry nor infantry, which I said was, without cause, falling back, could now, when attacked in the rear of the left of its camp, be prevailed upon to advance to the point of the left which was thus threatened, or in part to reoccupy its former position in front, which the enemy from the opposite hills soon perceived to be deserted, and in consequence again attacked, but fortunately without success, from the exertion of troops which were brought up from other quarters.

In this most extraordinary revolution, this most unlooked-for and cruelly mortifying reverse of fortune, where troops which should have felt most elated appeared all at once (I speak of this quarter of a very extended position) dismayed and subdued, it was found necessary to request

D

of General Lestoc (who was supposed, and reported to General Bennigsen, to be actually in the rear of his camp) to advance towards the front, to impose, by the appearance of his infantry, upon the enemy. But Lestoc was at this critical moment three English miles from us, and did not arrive before three o'clock. By this time the enemy had taken up a strong and formidable position on our left flank, in the rear of it ; and when a panic once seizes troops, your experience informs you how sadly distressing is the situation of the general commanding. The enemy could at first, without much loss, have been compelled to abandon his new position ; but by the time Lestoc arrived, he had made it a very strong one. It extended beyond the extremity of our left flank, occupying two small woods, which were about equally distant from his centre ; the whole of this space was filled with tirailleurs, etc. The enemy did not, however, advance ; he only cleared that part of our position by his guns, having placed himself in a most formidable position, in accomplishing which I cannot but think he displayed great military proficiency, by which he deprived us of the hitherto commanding advantage of our situation in front, and which he could not have accomplished but by the best organized troops. He never ceased occupying our attention in front with his light corps, having also pushed some troops to the right of our front, who menaced us occasionally. Lestoc came into our camp by our right with about thirteen thousand men. He immediately directed himself by our rear to the left, and advanced in two lines upon the right of the new position of the enemy, while the Russians advanced against them on the other extremity, and also towards his centre. The enemy appeared inclined to advance through our camp from left to right ; but there was no light for this, and the thing terminated in an affair of sharp shooting from and against the woods, and mutual exchange of great guns, by which some valuable lives were lost.

The day closed, leaving the enemy in his new position. At night the enemy opened a battery upon us rather on our right, which, we were informed, was done by the corps of Bernadotte.

The artillery ammunition had been suffered to be most unnecessarily and uselessly expended. The Russian chiefs were early cautioned not to permit this. The army had not been well fed for some days. They had fought well for some days, during which they had sustained great fatigue and privations of every kind, and during the greater part of this day they had displayed most undaunted courage, and had in every instance foiled the enemy in his attacks, and gained the superiority over him, except in man- œuvring, in which he showed most signal talent. (I allude to this new position, which he conceived as a great general and executed with the greatest precision and ability.) We were still in possession of the field of battle ; yet it was resolved to fall back, which we did during the night, leaving Lestoc, who had taken up a position, to cover the retreat. The Russians are at about nine miles from hence, and ten from where they fought. I don't hear that Lestoc has been attacked, or that the French advance in any direction. Though the French may not have lost in the long fight of yesterday a great number of men, yet their loss must have been considerable and the dismay of the troops great indeed, for undoubtedly the Russians have not the smallest dread of them, and that they know. The Russian army, on the other hand, are for the moment nearly disorganized— at least, in a most astonishing state of confusion, not unlike that which one occasionally sees in a Turkish army. Still I doubt not that a sufficient number can be collected to enable the superior officers, who are a fine set of fellows, and possessed of a most indignant feeling against the French, to make another very formidable resistance against Bonaparte, should he wish to persevere. He certainly ought to feel greatly mortified by the frequent and decisive repulses he experienced yesterday, and the resistance which a very superior number of his troops met for several days from a very small rear-guard of the Russians.

The loss on both sides yesterday must have been very considerable, though not so much as should have been, considering the number of hours we were engaged—from half-past six till half-past nine. I don't take any account of a few night bloody scenes which followed. The wounded are badly off. What we witnessed in that way was dreadfully affecting.

Sir C. Wilson's and my obligations to Bennigsen and his officers are great. A very good horse of his, which I rode yesterday, was badly wounded in two places. All the villages we have passed through have been ruined, as must be expected. The action yesterday destroyed several.

I have come into Königsberg for the night, but shall return to-morrow.

[Monday night, half-past five.

LETTER XX.

Memel, February 18th, 1807.

* The enclosed is a letter from Mr. Hutchinson to Lord Hutchinson. The battle of which it gives the details is said to have been extremely bloody. It is supposed the Russians

* Early in 1807 the eyes of Europe were turned to the Baltic coast. A great contest was to be decided between the Emperor of Russia and the King of Prussia, who were supported by Sweden and Great Britain on the one hand, and Bonaparte, supported by the populations of Italy, Spain, Holland,

and Prussians lost twenty thousand, and the French more. Since that time nothing of consequence has happened. The Russian head-quarters are at Königsberg, where the number of wounded officers is eight hundred.

We are quite ignorant of Bonaparte's intentions. An aide-de-camp of his, General Bertrand,* came here the day before yesterday and saw the king. What his object was has not yet been made known to Lord Hutchinson. He stayed one day only. Poor Wynne, we hear, has been ship-wrecked in Sweden. Lord Hutchinson has been very unfortunate with respect to his despatches, as none of the vessels which had them on board have made their passage good.

I sent to you a short time ago a gown of the queen's for the sake of the measure ; you will keep the original, and show your taste in those you send her.

The uncertainty of communication is very tiresome, as one has not half the pleasure in writing one would have if one were certain of one's letters arriving. I fear I have lost one or two of yours. Give my love to my father and Char., etc.

Ever yours very affectionately,

GOWER.

I very often wish you were here. You might, among other things, pick up amber on the seashore. *The queen* gave me two pieces she picked up the other day. I will give one to Char. when I see her.

and a great part of Germany. The French claimed the victory at Eylau, but their advantages were counterbalanced by the facility afforded to the manœuvres of a Swedish army between Dantzig and Hamburgh. It was anticipated that Bonaparte's distance from his resources in a region where his soldiers were unused to the climate would bring great privation to his army, but this season was a mild one, and the Russian organization was defective.

* Bertrand had already been to see Bennigsen with pacific overtures, but the Russian commander had replied that he was "sent by his master not to negotiate, but to fight." He came with the same overtures to the King of Prussia.

LETTER XXI.

Memel, March 7th, 1807.

MEINE LIEBE MUTTER,

The French have not retreated behind the
Vistula, and seem not disposed to be driven behind by
the combined forces, as they are complete masters of the
river passages.   The dead on the field of battle at Preussisch Eylau remain unburied, and seem likely, for the want
of hands to bury them, to remain so till spring, which is a
shocking circumstance.   The misery of all the surrounding
country is said to be inconceivable—villages without inhabitants—and God knows how long this state of things
may last ; but it seems thought that peace is not improbable.

Lord Hutchinson has received no communications from
Government for a long time, which, as the Baltic has been
open during the whole winter, *is very* extraordinary.   The
last letter I received from you was written two days before
Lord Hutchinson left England.   However, a vessel must
come in a day or two, and I must have a letter by it.   I
am very busily occupied at present with learning German,
and hope that you are able by this time to read pretty
fluently any Latin book that falls in your way.   We have
received some English papers up to the 21st of February,
by which I see that you are all well, and that you go
sometimes to Woolmer's, etc.   I shall enjoy receiving a
letter from you very much.   You would be much amused to
see and hear Lord Hutchinson when he is with the king and
queen, and the answers he makes them divert them a good
deal sometimes.   The *only* servant that he has is a little
stumpy footman, and his aide-de-camp, Colonel Eustace,
and Hervey, his secretary, have each a groom, and that
is the whole of their domestic establishment.   The weather

is as cold almost as it has been during the whole winter,
which has been an extremely mild one; but the climate
here is a very bad one, as the weather changes every hour.

How does Rugantino? They say Lord Douglas is
magnificence itself. The house that Lord Granville had is
much too small for him, and he has furnished another in
a very grand manner. The emperor is expected here soon.
I am determined to have a sledge at Trentham as soon
as I come back, as it is the pleasantest sort of promenade
possible. I go out in one every day here.

I hope my carriage is taken good care of, and that you
go out in it sometimes, as you have permission, you know.
I have not half the pleasure in writing to you that I should
have if I were certain that you would receive my letters,
but I think the chances are pretty equal.

The queen says that she should like nothing so much
as to make a tour in Scotland, in which case you are
engaged to do the honours of it to her.

Give my love to my pa and Char., etc. I expect a long
letter from her.

Ever affectionately yours,

GOWER.

LETTER XXII.

Memel, March 25th, 1807.

I am just returned from a little excursion to the Russian
head-quarters at Bartenstein, where I stayed two days and
saw a good many of the Russian generals. General
Bennigsen was very civil. Everything has remained quiet
lately, but great fears are entertained for Dantzig,* with

* In spite of the mild winter there was great sickness in the French army.
Bonaparte, therefore, in order to recover the *morale* of his troops by active
operations, decided to lay siege of Dantzig.

which all communication by land is nearly cut off. On the way back from Bartenstein, I saw the field of battle at Preussisch Eylau. Lord Hutchinson's brother, who has always been with the Russians, accompanied us to P. Eylau.

The dead are nearly all buried now, but many horses remain exposed. The poor town exhibits a *triste* appearance—most of the houses deserted, and bearing the marks of balls and bullets, as a great deal of fighting took place in the town. The whole road from Königsberg showed the marks of war. One was continually where the Russians or French had been—houses stripped of their timber, and entire villages without inhabitants. However, it was an interesting expedition, though, as we were not allowed to go to the avant postes, we did not see so much of the army as one might have wished. The king, etc., go in a few days to Georgenburg to see the guards pass. The emperor is expected, but it is not yet known exactly when. Many of the Russians wish for peace, but there is no doubt that they will fight well whenever the occasion offers ; but it must present itself, as Bennigsen has too much timid prudence to act with great energy, and in manœuvring the French, of course, have the advantage. We are very anxious to have accounts from England, where there seems a conspiracy to let us have neither public nor private news. I met General Victor at Königsberg, who, you know, was taken prisoner by some of the runaways and peasants. He is to be exchanged for Blucher. I should like to be able to fly over to you for an hour or so, to see how you all do.

Does Rugantino ever come near you ?

Merchant ships begin to come in in considerable numbers, yet we never receive any letters. However, *le bon temps viendra.* I hope you receive sometimes some from me, though I never expect one-half to get to the place of their destination.

Ever yours very affectionately,

GOWER.

If there were any plants or shrubs here, I would send you some to give to Mr. Butt, but there is nothing but sand.

LETTER XXIII.

Königsberg, April 15th, 1807.

I cannot tell you how happy I was some days ago to receive your letter by Baron Eben. It is the first I have received since Lord Hutchinson left England, and I was delighted to find that I had anticipated your wishes by staying with Lord Hutchinson, and the confirmation of my own idea that it would not be necessary for me to return by August has removed a little annoyance at the time, passed nearly in one place, not allowing to see a little more *of the world* before my return. The last letter I wrote to you was after an expedition I had made to the Russian head-quarters at Bartenstein, which, though very agreeable, has been surpassed by the one from which I am now returning, viz. to a small village on the Memel river called Kydullen, where the emperor, king, and queen, and grand-duke have been for some days, to see the Russian guards pass. Lord Hutchinson did not go, but a courier arriving from England the day after the party had set out (which courier brought *no* letter from you, by-the-by) gave me the excuse of taking a letter to the king, and I stayed four days, dining every day with the aforesaid emperor, king, queen, etc. ; and now the emperor and king have gone to Schippenbick, a place close to the Russian head-quarters, and they have sent for

Lord Hutchinson. But I hear news have been received at Memel of changes in the ministry, which have detained him a day or two there longer, in expectation of a messenger arriving. The queen and other people, among whom I and all such as return to Memel, have been obliged to make an enormous *détour* by this place, as the Memel, which allowed us to pass, is now unfrozen, and such mud, such roads as we have come through, are not to be imagined. All the court here are as civil and kind to me as possible, in spite of which I must say the king cuts a very unroyal figure, being extremely shy, and that the contrast between him and the emperor is great.

A *changement* has taken place in the ministry since the emperor's arrival. Hardenberg has succeeded to Zastrow, of which I approve.

20th.

I have had no opportunity yet of sending my letter. The emperor and king are at the head-quarters, Bartenstein. Lord Hutchinson goes to-morrow ; I continue here. We expect daily a messenger. Of course Lord Hutchinson won't stay here under the new people. We have no idea what they will do at head-quarters, whether they mean to fight or negotiate. The queen remains here a short time longer with her sister, the Princess of Solms, and one goes there almost every evening from seven till nine, but the evening before last was the pleasantest possible. The party consisted of the queen and her sister, the Prince of Orange, who is a very gentlemanlike man, one *dame d'honneur*, and myself. The queen and princess sang and played on the guitar, and, in short, to our great surprise, nine o'clock struck eleven times.

I hope you have not forgot the morning dress. If you could send any good new English songs for the queen, you would do well.

I hear that Rugantino has declared himself an enemy
to slavery. Though I shall be extremely glad to see you
all again, I like being abroad exceedingly.

I have not yet received your letters by Petersburg.

Ever yours affectionately,

GOWER.

LETTER XXIV.

Königsberg, April 27th, 1807.

I was made happy yesterday by the arrival of Jackson,
with two letters from you and two from Char., and the
two books, and your etchings, for all which many thanks.

We are all extremely sorry for the change, and agree in
opinion that it cannot continue, but the mischief which
may be the consequence cannot be too much regretted.
However, we trust that no efforts will be spared to make
the bed of roses as pleasant as one could wish.   I wrote a
letter a week ago, giving an account of an expedition to
see the guards pass at Kydullen.   Lord Hutchinson is now
at Bartenstein with their Majesties.

The queen is much obliged to you for the trouble you
have had about her dresses ; they have not yet arrived, but I
expect them every day.   I have another commission now,
but expressly for Char.—at her desire, as she says.   You
must have had enough already, and will vote her a bore.
I write now *de provision*, as I am expecting despatches from
Lord Hutchinson to forward directly, so I must be prepared.
I am afraid you must find my letters extremely dull and
insipid in comparison of what they ought to be, coming
from so far from you, and so near everything interesting
here ; but the truth is that nothing in the military way has
been done for some time, as the state of the roads has
prevented all operations.

We are extremely anxious about Dantzig, as they begin now to press it very closely.

The Russians, from all accounts, are terribly in want of money. I will enclose Bennigsen's *rapport* of the battle. By-the-by, I had almost forgot to say that on my happening to show your etchings this morning to the queen, she said she should like very much to have a drawing from you, so I hope you won't be angry if I am the cause of giving you that trouble. I would recommend one of Dunrobin. The weather is now delightful, and, if it continues for a few days, will enable the armies to begin again. It is feared that Austria will not declare till the Russians have gained some decisive advantage, and it is feared that the French rein-forcements lately have been very great. However, a very good spirit reigns, and great unanimity, they say. I saw a letter from the Prince of Wales to Lord Hutchinson the other day, in which he speaks of me in the kindest manner possible. I suppose, of course, it was intended for my perusal.

I am very glad to hear that my father is so well, and, in short, such good accounts of all of you. Nothing delights me so much as hearing from you, so don't lose any opportunity, please. There are some days that I can speak French pretty well, and others when I cannot explain myself in the least; I should like to know if the same thing used to be the case with you at Paris.

A prophet has appeared here lately, and caused some impression here. He is a common peasant, who has come all the way from *Heidelberg* in consequence of the orders of God, who has appeared four times to him, ordering him to come to Königsberg, where he should find the Emperor of Russia and King of Prussia, and that he is to have an audience of the king to tell him that Bonaparte in three months will disappear, that France is to be divided into three kingdoms, but that the King of Prussia and his people must become more pious and virtuous.

The peasant, who is a plain, honest-looking man, refused three times, but the fourth was frightened into complaisance. He says that all that happened at Austerlitz was foretold to him last year, and he informed his neighbours. When you read this to my father he will say " Pooh!" and you will wish that you could believe it.

Ever affectionately yours,
Gower.

April 29th.

Eight thousand Russians and Prussians are now marching through this place to relieve Dantzig.

Letter XXV.

Königsberg, May 20th, 1807.

Nothing has taken place between the armies yet. Bennigsen has not attacked them, though they (the French) have been obliged to send a good number of their men to Dantzig, in consequence of the Russian and Prussian expedition to that place, which I mentioned in my last letter to you. It consisted of about seven or eight thousand men. They attempted to relieve Dantzig by attacking the French near the " Fier Wasser " (that is where the Vistula empties itself into the sea), but from a want of good management, and from the ships we have there not being able to get up the river far enough to be of any assistance, they have failed, though they fought with the greatest possible bravery ; but the numbers they had to contend with exceeded their own so much, from continual reinforcements crossing the river, that they were obliged to retreat under the guns of the fort, after losing about fifteen hundred, and losing a good many officers. It is thought almost impossible for Dantzig to hold out much longer, as they are much pressed and want ammunition.* Its loss will be a great loss to us. We expect Lord Granville here daily. I have reason to think he will find his business very unpleasant, as the Russians have neither money nor provisions, and are in want of everything. Lord Hutchinson is to leave this place to-morrow to go to Stralsund to consult with the King of Sweden. He expects to return in ten days.

The Emperor of Russia has been extremely civil to him, and took a liking to him from the beginning.

I am extremely impatient for Granville's arrival, as I suppose he will bring me letters, which I cannot tell you how happy I am to receive. The morning dresses have not yet arrived ; I suppose they are waiting for a messenger. As Lord Hutchinson's is chiefly a military mission, he thinks he cannot return till something has been done. You can have no idea how impatient they are here for our expedition, which seems to be looked on as everything now. Bonaparte has been in person before Dantzig, but has now returned to Finckenstein.† Bennigsen's patience seems very, very great. Lord Pembroke is also expected here. I hope they will not come in the same ship, that I may have letters by both. *Oh joy, joy!*

Char. told me before I left England that she should expect me to come home a very polished person, much improved, which I have some fear she will not find the case, as I have not seen many persons with good manners

---

* Dantzig finally surrendered after a siege of fifty-two days, on May 27th, the garrison being allowed to march out to Königsberg.

† It was from the camp at Finckenstein that Bonaparte wrote to the Senate that he had instituted Duchies as rewards for eminent services, Marshal Le Febure being created Duke of Dantzig.

and good *ton* since I left you, except the queen, who is perfect in every respect ; and I have some little doubts of the state of civilization *elsewhere*, from the examples I have seen. The queen is still here; she lives at her sister's, and people may go to tea there, which I do every evening. It is very agreeable, as she is very agreeable, and some- times, when there are few people, she plays and sings ; and, once a week or so, I am invited to stay to supper. She is very glad to be able to throw off a little of the *gêne* and dulness in which she is generally obliged to live, so takes the advantage of having neither the king nor her *grande maîtresse* here to live socially and pleasantly; but I am afraid this will not last long, as the king will very soon probably return to Memel, and she with him, and he does not like society, therefore she cannot have it.

My letters are always so stupid to be sent from such a distance ; however, they let you know that I exist, which is something. Give my love to pa, Char., Eliz., etc.

Ever yours most affectionately,

GOWER.

LETTER XXVI.

Memel, Wednesday, June 17th, 1807.

If our public news here were not unfortunately so bad, I should be extremely happy at this moment, having just received from Lord Granville * a great many letters from you, etc. ; but, alas ! Königsberg is taken, and Bennigsen by this time on this side of the river Memel, after having received a most woeful defeat. After gaining, as we heard, a brilliant victory at Heilsberg,† the next news was that

* First Earl Granville, the uncle of the writer, and Ambassador to Russia.

† This " brilliant victory " was only a momentary check of the French army.

the French were advancing towards Königsberg, and
Bennigsen obliged to retreat to endeavour to save it ;
and yesterday came the account that, after as good a
defence as General Lestocq was able to make, a capitulation was necessary, and Prince Murat at six o'clock on
Monday evening entered in triumph (I left it on Friday
to join Lord Granville here, but he did not return from
Tilsit, where he had been to the emperor, who is now gone
to Wilna, till last night), and Bennigsen the same day
received a complete defeat near Tassiava (?).* Thirty thousand Russians are either killed, wounded, or run away ; at
the same time the French loss must have been great, for
the Russians fought well; they only want a good commander, but from one who has always lost his head after
what he has called victories, what can one expect after a
defeat ? Preparations are making to leave this, as it will
not be safe to remain long. What a melancholy thing for
the poor queen and all to be obliged to emigrate ! Riga
will be the next place of refuge.

On arriving here on Friday evening, the first person
I saw was the queen, who was delighted with the good
news of the victory at Heilsberg, which she had just
received from the king from Tilsit ; and on Saturday I
and one or two English that came with Lord Granville
accompanied her to the *Astrea* frigate, where we were all
very sick and very jolly, and as the captain could not
talk one word of French, I did the honours to her, and
we passed one of the pleasantest days possible, little expecting that in two days we should receive such a melancholy account. I have not yet heard anything of Lord
Hutchinson, who is with General Bennigsen.

I am extremely happy at having Lord Granville and at
hearing that I may stay the winter ; though I shall, never-

* This seems to refer to the French victory at Friedland.

theless, be very, very, very happy to see you all again, and I am delighted to hear such good reports of your healths.

I have been reading your letters over and over with great pleasure, and am always sorry when I come to the end of them. The queen is extremely pleased with the gowns : she wore the plainest of them this evening ; the other two, she says, are too good for her at present, but she likes them very much. Memel is overflowing with fugitives from Königsberg. The queen says that she is much consoled by the idea that she has always done what she has conceived her duty, and had rather live on potatoes than be in any way subservient to Bonaparte. She behaves extremely well on this melancholy occasion. You islanders will now begin to have a little leisure to think of us here, as for some time you have been so occupied at home that you have thought very little of us foreigners, which apathy, I can assure you, meets with anything but praise. Many a good time have I been attacked on this subject by all ranks from the highest, as people on these occasions like to scold those they can have an opportunity of scolding, without considering the justice or injustice of such behaviour ; however, I always think it very natural for them to do so, and soothe them as well as I can. Of course, Lord Granville will very soon send another courier, and I will not let the opportunity go by.

Ever yours affectionately,

GOWER.

Give my love to my father. I am constantly wishing that you were here. The queen says she will write to thank you for the trouble you have taken for her—before she leaves this, if she can. She is *très reconnaissante*.

E

LETTER XXVII.

Memel, June 24th, 1807.

Mr. Hervey, Lord Hutchinson's private secretary, is to leave Memel—perhaps in an hour, and perhaps in a week—so that I must prepare, as I do not mean to lose so good an opportunity.

I received a letter from you and one from Char. since those brought by Lord Granville, for which many thanks to both, and also for the music that accompanied it. General Bennigsen is on this side the Memel river, nearly opposite Tilsit, in and about which the French are. Lord Hutchinson, etc., have come hither from him for a few days. They describe the battles of Heilsberg and Friedland to have been very bloody, and General Bennigsen a man very incapable of commanding a large army, especially against such an enemy. With another general at the head things might yet go on, but Lord Hutchinson is very gloomy and hopeless on the occasion. Moreover, an armistice, we are hearing, has been concluded, and peace, I suppose, will be talked of directly. Whether the French will offer propositions that can possibly be accepted remains to be seen. The emperor, who had gone to Wilna to meet some of the reinforcements, and the king are going to Tourlagen, about four German miles from Tilsit,* to consult together. I suppose Lord Granville will go to them there.

Lord Hutchinson has been recalled, but means to stay to see the affair out, after which he talks of returning home through Russia and Sweden. I am extremely glad for myself that Lord Granville has come, as it will make much difference to me in Russia. He wrote to you a few days

---

* Bonaparte entered Tilsit on June 19th, the Emperor of Russia and the King of Prussia retiring in great haste.

ago. They find him more amiable than Lord Hutchinson here, which is not surprising, all things considered.

Pray send your book for the queen as soon as it is finished ; I am very impatient to see it. I cannot tell you how much longer we shall stay here, as, if war lasts, that will depend, I suppose, on the French ; and if peace is made, I suppose the emperor, and of course Lord Granville, etc., will go straight to Petersburg.

I am glad that you have received my letters. A good number of them have been given to gentlemen to take charge of, which is not the most expeditious way in general ; but when they go with despatches I always fear they may be opened, which is unpleasant, though there has never, I believe, been any treason in any of them—no popery!

The Newcastle people are very ungrateful to give so much trouble after all our civilities. I suppose it will not be necessary for me to ride over to pay Sir P—— and Master Fletcher a visit another time? Pray give G. Vernon my compliments, and say that he may expect an answer very soon.

June, Friday.—The armistice has been concluded—a week's notice to be given before a renewal of hostilities. The emperor and king have met Bonaparte on the river,* and had two long conferences and embraces. We do not know the result. I suppose we shall be going to Petersburg, as the emperor will probably not stay while negotiations are going on. Harvey is just going.

Ever yours very affectionately,

GOWER.

The dresses are liked extremely by the queen and everybody, and your taste much approved of.

---

* A raft was constructed on the Niemen for the meeting. An armistice was arranged ; half the town of Tilsit was made neutral ground, and a period of feasting and mutual entertainment ensued.

My love to Char., and I hope you have a great many
balls, etc. I am very glad to hear that eyes are so well.
Adieu.

LETTER XXVIII.

Memel, July 3rd, 1807.

Well, Bonaparte and the emperor are both at Tilsit,
where the former, I believe, does everything in his own
way, and we may take what care we can of ourselves in
England, as our great ally will do very little for us. They
say that they have sent from Tilsit a messenger overland
to London. The emperor has nobody with him of common
sense. Czartorisky, who is the best, is not there. The first
meeting on the bridge on the Memel would, from all
accounts, make an excellent caricature. It rained very hard,
and the two emperors and their attendants were obliged
to huddle together under a sort of awning for shelter, while
the King of Prussia was riding up and down on this bank
of the river, completely wet through. The king lives on
this side, but goes over to Tilsit every day. The emperor
lives there entirely, and Bonaparte also. The French army
is at a little distance, and the poor emperor has one battalion
of his guards there with him, so he is completely a sort
of hostage.

I hope the poor queen will not be obliged to go to be
presented to Bonaparte, as it would be a most cruel thing
for her; but I am afraid she will not escape this punishment,
though nothing has been done yet on the subject. It is
rather odd that while the king, etc., are living with Bonaparte fourteen German miles from hence, we should be
dining or drinking tea with her every day here. Lord
Granville's embassy at Petersburg will probably be rendered

much less pleasant than formerly, from some rascally French ambassador giving himself airs everywhere, and, indeed, for the English in general. I am very impatient to receive your book, as one's stay here is so uncertain, and I should be sorry to go before it comes, besides my wish to see it.

A Mr. Mackenzie, who came with Lord Granville, will take this. He was to have been with the army to send information from thence to [illegible], but, as unfortunately he can be no longer useful there, he is going back.

Yours most affectionately,

GOWER.

Give my love to everybody.

LETTER XXIX.

Memel, July 10th, 1807.

Peace,* if not signed to-day, will be concluded to-morrow, and the parties have left Tilsit. Bonaparte has gone to Königsberg, whence he is to proceed to Paris, some say through Dresden to pay his donations to the King of Saxony, to whom Prussian Poland is to be given.

We know very little yet of the terms, but to Prussia they are as bad as possible, as she is to lose almost everything. The visit which the poor queen has been obliged to make to Bonaparte has been a useless humiliation. In consequence of hints that her presence might give a more favourable turn to things (contrary to the advice of Hardenberg, who, by-the-by, is no longer minister), she was sent for, and, sacrificing all private feelings, went to Tilsit,

* The treaty was actually concluded on July 7th between Napoleon and Alexander of Russia, whereby Prussia was reduced to the position of a secondary power, which she held before the partition of Poland in 1772.

where she dined twice with Bonaparte. She went first to the king's quarters there, where Bonaparte came and invited her to dinner. He was as polite as possible for him to be, though the beginning of his conversation was rather singular. After admiring her dress, he said, "On dit, madame, que vous aimez beaucoup la toilette." She had a long *tête-à-tête* with him, which only seemed to encourage false hopes. He said the next day he should not give anything for the *beaux yeux* of the queen, who in consequence treated him at the second dinner as coldly as she could. It is plain that his object in holding out any little hope before was to give her the personal mortification of visiting such a devil as he is. Do you remember an expedition to the *Astrea* frigate that I told you of? About a week ago we made a second, when Lord Granville, etc., were of the party. Soon after, Bonaparte said to the king, "While we negotiate here, and you are requesting of me to give you back some provinces, the queen, with a party of English, goes on board an English frigate. If she chooses to have them for her friends, let them help her; I'll not give up an inch." Is not this truly worthy of his great, heroic mind? Remember that, if we do make peace with him—and Russia is to make us do so, they say—remember that I have sworn I will never be presented to him, in spite *of any scolding* I may get on the subject, as I was once before at Cassiobury. If ever I am, you may consider me as inconsequent and weak as the Emperor of Russia—the great Alexander—who, I believe, sees by this time what a goose and fool Bonaparte has made of him. He, our great and noble ally, after making a separate peace, is to join against us if we will not agree to Bonaparte's offers. They say he is to have Moldavia and Wallachia; for, as Bonaparte said, "The Turks have deceived both you and me—why should not we take from them what ought to belong to us?" It is said, too, to make the thing complete, that the King of Sweden, on our landing, has declared his armistice at an end, and is to commence hostilities on the 13th. A pretty time to choose, with his handful of men, to fight against all the French, etc., who have nothing else on their hands! Jerome Bonaparte is to be King of Westphalia.* Murat behaved very kindly at Tilsit, saying that he was extremely sorry for Bonaparte's harshness; that, as for himself, his only wish was to live quietly at Paris, and that he was quite unfit for the part that Bonaparte wished him to take. Bonaparte wished the emperor very much to take as far as the Memel river, which he has, however, refused.

The Emperor of Russia is on his road to Petersburg. Lord Granville has received no official intimation yet of his departure, but expects it every moment, as they can hardly treat us so cavalierly as to leave him without a word. We shall probably set off as soon as he receives it, which I the less regret as I suppose they would find themselves here obliged to be rather shy of us, for they say that Bonaparte hears everything that the queen, etc., say.†

* By the Treaty of Tilsit, Jerome was acknowledged King of Westphalia, Joseph King of Naples, and Louis King of Holland.

† Writing on the 31st of July, 1807, to Kirkpatrick Sharp, my father's mother says, "We heard from Gower yesterday; still with Lord Granville at Memel, but expecting every moment to set out for St. Petersburg. He is in a rage at the late events that have happened, and his sentiments for the Queen of Prussia revives in one's mind that of Lord Craven and Sir Henry Wooton for the unfortunate Queen of Bohemia, by whom such respectful adoration was carried to its utmost extent. He must soon come here to assist in defending us from the invasion, as his services can be no longer required on the Continent; and he seems disposed to exert himself with all the enthusiasm such an occasion will demand, for Bonaparte declares he will be in England in a year."

Letter XXX.

July 11th.

The messenger is to go this evening. We have been walking with the king and queen this morning. She is looking extremely ill and melancholy, as you may suppose. They will be obliged to stay here for some time, as the French troops are not to march off yet, in order to be able to spoil the harvest and create a famine in the country, in which there is no doubt they will succeed. They have destroyed sixteen villages to make their camp near Tilsit, which, however, is a thing to see from its regularity and situation. Whenever Bonaparte rode out with the emperor and king it was always *ventre à terre*, that he might take the lead. He says he will be master of England in a year. We shall see.

Yours ever affectionately,

Gower.

I will write as soon as I hear the particulars of the peace.* The Prussian one was signed yesterday; the Russian the day before.

Goltz, the Prussian minister, was making objections to some articles, on which Bonaparte took him by the shoulder and said, "Ce n'est pas à vous à négocier avec moi; c'est à moi à dicter; je suis le vainqueur." Goltz went out of the room, saying that he could not sign; but when the Russian one was signed, and Prussia deserted and left to herself, there was no help. She keeps Silesia.†

* One of the articles of the treaty with Prussia was that, until the ratification of a definitive peace between England and France, all the ports of Prussia were to be closed against the English.

† The restoration of Silesia to Prussia by the pacification of Tilsit was looked upon in Europe as an example of Bonaparte's Machiavellian policy, as it was calculated that the possession of the Duchy of Prussia would be a constant source of hostility between the courts of Berlin and Vienna, just as

LETTER XXXI.

Memel, August 27th, 1807.

I have had no opportunity of sending a letter for a long time, as we have had no minister here to send despatches ; but now Mr. Garlike has arrived, though as yet he remains merely a traveller, and not a public person. However, be that as it may, Mr. Jackson is to return to England and to be the bearer of this letter ; and I hope he won't open my letter, as I am just going to say that I am very glad the ministry have not sent his brother as minister here, where he is by no means popular, and I think they might have spared the Prince Royal of Denmark the double insult of making such a demand by such a vulgar, disagreeable man, as from all reports Mr. Jackson is. We have not yet heard the result of the Danish business. It will furnish Bonaparte with many pretexts for his future conduct, whatever the result may be.*

The condition of the Prussians is very lamentable, as the French have not the least regard for their treaty. Every day brings the account of fresh demands and new difficulties. They seem to have not the least idea of retiring till they have completely ruined the country, which they are doing by every possible means. They are even apprehensive here that Berlin may yet be taken from them.

I have received no letters from you for a long time. Mr. Garlike says that he forwarded some to me lately. The vessel on which they were was probably afraid of

the military highway across Silesia would foment jealousy between the courts of Berlin and of Dresden.

* After the battle of Friedland, Sweden alone remained faithful to the English alliance. Denmark affected a neutrality which she was incapable of maintaining, and requested the British Government to be excused from receiving our shipping at the ports of Sleswig and Holstein. After protracted negotiations, an English fleet and army were sent to the Baltic, and Copenhagen was bombarded.

entering the port, and has gone to some other place with them. The shutting up of the ports has not yet been put into effect, but the French may send to-morrow to insist on its immediate execution, and then, of course, it must be done without delay, or they will come themselves. The country has suffered much worse from them as friends than when they were enemies, and they have no prospect of being delivered from this state of things.

We have had an extraordinarily hot summer in this part of the world, and it still continues so, so much that I am obliged to take off my coat to write, being tormented by *heat-drops.* I am very impatient for the arrival of your book and of the stockings, all the which are anxiously expected. I hope you have escaped your sneezing fits, and that the eyes have continued well. You ought to send me something for my birthday. I suppose you were not in time for Newcastle Races * this year? By-the-by, I must write to G. Vernon, over whom the Lichfield Races are at present impending. I do not envy him, but I hope nothing will happen to deprive you of *the pleasure* of going to them this year. I intend to leave this place on Sunday (to-day being Thursday, 28th), so that I must tell Mr. Garlike to give any parcel that may come for me to the queen. I shall find all your old letters of the winter at Petersburg. I should like very much to be able to walk over and pay you a visit, and see the improvements at Trentham. I heard some weeks ago that Wood had some intentions of passing part of the next winter at Petersburg, but I have not since heard if he has put, is putting, or will put his travelling designs into execution. Pray give my compliments to Mr. Butt.† The time seems to have passed very

* Newcastle-under-Lyme, near Trentham.

† Mr. Butt was for many years the Vicar of Trentham, and a close friend of my family.

fast since I left you, but when one considers half the things
that have happened since, it appears a long time.*

I shall pay my respects to his French Majesty at
Mittau in passing. Mrs. Bootle's letter to the Empress
of Russia will have become of a certain age before she
receives it. I have found this place much more agreeable
on account of there being no English ; but at Petersburg,
I believe, they swarm. I have just finished reading Corinne,
which has given me a very great desire to see Italy, though,
by-the-by, it is a desire I have always had. But, unfortunately, one cannot always have one's way in the world, so
I must content myself with the cold Russian winter. I
dream very often that I am with you, which is very pleasant,
and I am now going to bed with that intention.

Ever most affectionately yours,
GOWER.†

* Louis XVIII.

† As this is the last letter written from Memel by my father, I think it
will be of interest to insert here a copy of a remarkable letter written to him
by Queen Louise. It evidently alludes to a letter from my father written to
the Countess Voss on the character of the queen herself. She writes as follows :
" Vous voulez scavoir mes idées sur la lettre à la Comtesse Voss—les voilà.—
Elle doit être très flattée de tout ce que vous lui dites d'obligeant et de flatteur ;
l'opinion avantageuse que vous avez d'elle ne peut lui être indifferent, mais
une reflection surtout doit être la dominante. Tout ce bon prestige de beauté,
de grâce, de perfection que vous voyez dans la Comtesse se disseperont bientôt,
si vous ne la croyez pas en même temps très bonne, et si vous n'étiez pas persuadé de ses avantages moraux, comme vous le lui avez remarqué si souvent.
Voilà ce qui surtout doit pénétrer la Comtesse d'une vive réconnaissance et je
suis sûre que c'est cela, à qui elle sera le plus sensible, et qu'elle n'oubliera de
sa vie. Elle doit encore sentir qu'elle n'est pas aussi bonne, aussi vertueuse
que votre bonté et excellente nature vous porte à la croire, mais cela sera pour
elle toujours un grand aiguillon, un véritable encouragement de s'améliorer
autant que cela sera dans son pouvoir, âfin de répondre à la haute opinion que
vous avez d'elle. Que la Comtesse sera heureuse si elle pourrait se dire avec
verité avoir contribué à vous faire aimer et respecter son sexe, et si elle avoit
pu vous persuader qu'au milieu du monde on peut conserver une simplicité de
mœurs, une certaine pureté d'esprit et de goût, qui provient surtout d'un fond
de religion et de principes vertueux. Oui, my lord, soyez persuadé qu'il y a
encore des femmes respectables ; et surtout persuadez vous de plus en plus que
la vertu n'est pas un fantôme, et que c'est le seul bonheur des cœurs honnêtes
d'y croire et de la pratiquer. Puisse le souvenir de la Comtesse avoir toujours

Letter XXXII.

Mittau, September 2nd, 1807.

Of course this letter will not go from me till I arrive at Petersburg ; but I cannot help beginning it now, as I am just come from talking a good deal about you.   I told you in my letter from Memel last week that I should be presented to the King of France in passing this place, but this has not been in my power, as, to my great surprise, yesterday on the road I met a large cavalcade of carriages, which, I heard, was his Majesty on his way to pay a visit to the King of Sweden.   However, the queen and the Duchesse d'Angoulême remain here; and this morning I went to the Duc d'Avray, and told him how desirous I was to pay my respects.   He said that he did not think I should be able to see the queen, as she was very unwell, but he would go and see.   In a few minutes he returned, saying that she was extremely sorry not to be able to see me, but that she was obliged to keep her bed, and that the Duchesse d'Angoulême would be very glad to see me directly; on which we went to the Duchesse de Serent, and with her to the duchesse, who began directly to talk about you—that I was *like you*, how grateful they all are to you for your attention, and about your lending my clothes to her brother.*   And she all but cried; I believe she had before I came into the room, as the Duc d'Avray said that his mentioning me had affected *her much*.

une heureuse influence sur votre existence, et vous retirer d'actions qui ne s'accorderaient pas avec votre manière de penser ; c'est alors seulement qu'elle auroit un droit à s'enorgueiller, car il n'y à rien de plus doux que de se dire d'avoir contribuèe au bonheur de quelqu'un qu'on *estime*. La Comtesse qui reconnoit sûrement en vous les avantages d'un 'pure heart,' et d'un 'good nature' fera toujours des vœux pour que vous trouverez le bonheur en conservant ces avantages qui sont les véritables bienfaits du ciel."

* The unfortunate Louis XVII.

She afterwards said she hoped I would stay and dine, which, of course, I did not refuse ; and after the dinner, which was a very pleasant one, the queen sent to say she would see me, when I found a little woman, with gray hair, talking a great deal and very fast. The visit did not last long ; but afterwards I had again a long conversation with the duchesse, who is really a very charming person—something like Gertrude,* not so handsome and not so shy. She desired me to send her compliments to you, and express her regard for you, which, you see, I lose no time in doing.

I left Memel the day before yesterday, and came here without stopping. Part of the country I have come through is very beautiful—too flat, but well wooded and cultivated. The capital is not situated in the best part of it, and the *séjour* at the palace, which is very large but ruinous, must be very *triste*. Lady Ossulstone's sister † is here, but not visible. I am not sure whether she has just been, or is to be, brought to bed, which I own is stupid enough ; but I believe it is the first.

LETTER XXXIII.

Petersburg, September 27th, 1807.

On arriving here I found your letter of the 24th of July. We are at a small villa, almost in the river, about four versts from the town, into which we are to remove next week.

Lord Granville has a very fine, large house, where we shall all be comfortable enough. I have seen very little of Petersburg yet. Having heard so much of it, it was impossible to be surprised at its beauty and magnificence,

* Lady Gertrude Sloane-Stanley (*née* Howard), and aunt of my parents.
† A daughter of the Duc de Grammont.

which, though certainly great, did not exceed my expectations. ᛫ The only thing I have seen is the Hermitage, of
which one has heard so much. It is a very large house,
with a great many large rooms, filled with good and bad
pictures, and leaves no impression on one's mind afterwards.

I have seen very few people—none who seem remarkable in any way; but very few people are come to town
yet, so I will suspend all judgment till my next letter.
Lord Granville is very kind to me, and very agreeable, and I
am sure I shall be very *comfortable*, as one could wish with
him. The stockings arrived safe ; I sent them to Memel
yesterday. People here are very much afraid of our fleet,
and at the same time very much afraid of the French,
which they show by their civilities to M. Savary, to whom
they give balls, etc. God help them ! One winter of St.
Petersburg will perfectly content me, and I shall never
desire to come so far north again, unless I find them much
more agreeable than I expect. I shall go to Moscow when
the *trainage* sets in ; it begins to be very cold and wintry
already.

I have not yet been presented at court, and therefore
can give no opinion about the empress's. Of the emperor
I have seen enough already. We have just heard, by
American ships, of the temporary capitulation of Copenhagen. We do not seem to have been over-successful in
that scheme.

I will execute your commissions here as soon as possible,
as you deserve for having executed mine ; but you must
send the book as soon as it is finished and bound.

Give my love to my father and Char. I wrote to you
last from Memel a few days before I left it ; since that the
Prussian ports have been shut ; they are much to be pitied.
Lord Douglas is to set off to-morrow to Moscow, where he

means to stay some time. Lord Hutchinson had left this place for Stockholm a few days before I arrived. I suppose he was not enchanted with Petersburg, from his staying so short a time.

Ever yours affectionately,

GOWER.

LETTER XXXIV.

Petersburg, October 1st, 1807.

I am very glad I have come here, as it is always better to have ideas a little more fixed about places than one can have without having seen them, and the having been here will so entirely prevent all wishes of taking this journey again ; and it would have been a great pity to have lost so very good an opportunity as this is with Lord Granville, who makes it as pleasant as possible, and whom I like very much indeed. But if he were not here, and I had come here as soon as originally intended, I should, in a very short time, have seen everything worth seeing here—which, after all, is not much—and been off; for I must own I think the place offers as few inducements to keep one long as any place can well do. For, in the first place, after having read and heard so much of the magnificence of the buildings and the beauty of the town, when one comes to have a near inspection, one has soon seen enough of it. In short, my ideas of what a magnificent town should be are much grander and more magnificent than St. Petersburg ; and, in the second place, if you, who complain sometimes of the dulness of the society of London, were transported here, I do believe you would think the London society very good, and certainly far preferable, and would like parties and assemblies much better than what one finds here. The women have a sort of vanity, which keeps them always at home, except on grand occasions of birthdays, etc. ; and every one that has a house has one or two *dames de compagnie*, which, with half a dozen men (and the Russians in general have never read a book in their lives, and I believe most of them cannot read), form the society which you find whenever you are received. The men of fashion are the officers of the guards. In short, it is very bad. Add to this that the women are also in general very ugly.

We thought about a week ago that your *selfish* wishes would be gratified, and that you would soon have the satisfaction of seeing George, etc. ; but for the present, at least, that seems to have blown over, whether from the *magnanimous* being afraid that, as the frost has not yet set in, he may yet receive a visit for which the hero is not prepared, or whether from any other reason, remains to be seen. It is certain that he consults the thermometer very frequently, and is much more impatient this year for the promenades *en trainaux* than he was ever known to be before. They were very much inclined to show their teeth and growl about Copenhagen, so much so that it was thought right to give our merchant ships at Cronstadt a hint to sail as soon as they could, for fear of accidents ; but the Minister Romanzow yesterday swore to Lord Granville that *as yet* they have never had any idea of laying on.

If they do it now they will catch nothing, as all the ships are off. Experienced people say that it is really wonderful how much the Russians have lately found out the art of speaking freely their opinions in society. It certainly is not wonderful that their emperor should be much lowered in public opinion since his late achievements. If his sister, the Grand-Duchess Catherine, were on the throne, she would manage much better, they say,

I have not seen any of them yet; but she hates the French, and says so.

If you see Mrs. Bootle, tell her that I have given her letter for the empress to her *dame d'honneur*, Madame Protascoff. I have not yet been presented to her.

I have seen Madame de Tarente once ; she desired me to say many things to you. She is to go in a few days to Mittau. Good God! what a dismal place to pass the winter in! Lord Douglas is gone to Moscow, and thence means to go to Kieff, where, I believe, he will pass the winter. He has spent a great deal of money here in curiosities of all sorts.

I have not received any letter from you since one dated July 24th.

Yours very affectionately,
G.*

LETTER XXXV.

Petersburg, Sunday, October 10th, 1807.

I received the day before yesterday your letter of the 5th of September, and hope that before this you have received one or two letters from me since the one of July 11th.

I lost nothing by not coming here exactly as soon as Lord Granville, as nothing happened during that time, and the winter is much the best time to go to Moscow.

Bonaparte is continuing to behave as ill as possible to

---

* Of this letter, dated October 1st, 1807, my father writes, "Many of these observations must be considered as having been stated without sufficient acquaintance with the subject ; and, of course, the comparisons by a young traveller of his first impression of a society quite new to him, with that with which he was intimate, and consequently more at ease, must require allowance and excuse. It certainly was not a brilliant time for Russia."

F

the Russians.   At Königsberg lately an actor appeared on the stage in a French uniform, with the *Legion d'Honneur*, etc., which, as you may suppose, could not be agreeable to a Prussian audience—particularly to Prussian officers, of whom there were a good many present.   They indiscreetly, perhaps, but very naturally, showed their displeasure, and made him change the dress.   Bonaparte, on hearing this, sent to the king to say that, till he received satisfaction for this insult, the French troops shall not give up an inch of ground, and nothing shall be done.

The satisfaction he demands is that two of these officers shall *be shot*.   It is not yet known how this will end, but it is certainly a most shameful proceeding in Bonaparte.

The weather here is not at all calculated to put me in better humour with the Russians.   Ever since I wrote last to you we have had incessant rain.

The emperor is to go to-morrow to review his army; he is expected to be absent a fortnight.   I do not know whether General Savary means to accompany him or not. I have just now been very much amused by reading Lord Macartney's character of the Russians, in which there is certainly a great deal of truth in my opinion.

I am glad you have found a *good deal to do* at Trentham for my father's sake.   When I come home I suppose he will expect a great many hints from me for improvements; but if he does he will be disappointed, as far as Russia is concerned at least, for as to forming one's taste it can't do much.

Yours very affectionately,

GOWER.

LETTER XXXVI.

Petersburg, October 29th, 1807.

"Have you seen the comet?" is the usual question here now, which has made its appearance lately. I have just been looking at it, or rather for it, but am not able to tell you what it portends. The comet puts me in mind of an eclipse of the moon we saw once at Dunrobin, and the thought of that makes me say that I rejoice very much at your intention, and that I prefer going there to going to the Crimea, and am delighted with the thought of going there again with all of you. I begin to be impatient to see Moscow. The people there, from all accounts, are so much better worth seeing than these; they cannot be less, God knows.

The frost to-day seems to have serious thoughts of setting in, which I am glad of, as I wish to go to Moscow for two reasons; the first is that if I put off my journey thither, we may be sent off on the road before I am ready (though there is no particular reason for thinking so at this moment); and the second, that, as I have already told you, I have seen enough of this place. I have nothing particular, you see, to say to you at present, and write merely because there happens to be an opportunity for so doing, which, if I were to let pass, my conscience might perhaps give me some little stings for a day or two.

I hope you never read any part of my letters aloud at dessert, if Mr. Butt or anybody happen to dine. My father and Char. may, I believe, in. general be allowed to have the honour of hearing them without much fear of my reproaches, but none other. If the only object of one's travels were to find good society, that at Memel must be allowed to be ten hundred thousand times better than any to be found here, or, I believe, anywhere else, till one returns *chez soi, en comparaison.* We expect letters from England every day ; as soon as the boxes are opened, my eyes spy out your hand directly, if it be there.

Ever affectionately yours,

GOWER.

LETTER XXXVII.

Petersburg, November 8th, 1807.

This is probably the last letter you will receive from me, as that d——d fool the Emperor of Russia has thought fit to comply with Bonaparte's commands, and has finished his complete disgrace by declaring war with us, or, what amounts to the same thing, has, in the worst written note that ever minister penned, signified his imperial intention of recalling his ambassador from London, and of no longer having the honour of a British Embassy at Petersburg. This state of things cannot last long ; but he will repent, when too late perhaps.   As it is, they say that the measure is as unpopular a one here as one could wish.

I am sorry not to have seen Moscow, especially as I never, I hope, shall be so near it again ; for as to this place, I must own my regret will not hurt my health.

We shall probably go in four or five days, so you may be soon on the look-out.   Sir R. Wilson, who sets off this evening, will take this.

Ever yours affectionately,

GOWER.

LETTER XXXVIII.

Yarmouth Roads, January 8th, 1808.

I am as happy to tell you, as you can possibly be to hear it, that we have arrived here at last. We shall disembark to-morrow, and shall probably, I suppose, be in London late the day after, when I shall be very happy to see you all. I will then tell you of our having been a month on board, having been obliged to put back into Gottenburg, after tossing about for a week in the Schelde, etc., etc., etc.

Ever affectionately yours,

GOWER.

This series of letters concludes at an interesting point in the history of the Napoleonic wars. Bonaparte was at this moment master of the Continent of Europe, and Great Britain alone of the powers preserved a position of independence. In the interval of six years between the date of the last of these letters and the first of the second series the Peninsular Campaign took place ; the Empress Josephine was divorced, and Marie Louise became the wife of Bonaparte ; Russia was again invaded ; the disastrous retreat from Moscow brought about the uprising of Austria and Prussia, which powers united with Russia to throw off the yoke of Napoleon.

END OF PART I.

PART II.

PART II

LETTER I.

* Helvoet, December 17th, 1813, seven o'clock, Friday.

After a passage of above *fifty* hours, we have arrived safely here, and the first thing I do is to tell you of it.

We are all at, I believe, the only inn, and that is previously as full as it can hold, so that we passengers have not much chance of getting beds ; however, Nott is gone out to see.

Sir Thomas Graham has, we hear, landed in the Roon Pot, and is going to Wilhelmstadt to act against Begen-op-Zoom. A small detachment of the guards is here, on its way to join him.

We had a very tedious passage—two long nights, but not very windy. We left Harwich with a very fair wind, but, unluckily, a haze came on with the night, and prevented our seeing some lights off [illegible], and the captain of the *Lady Nepean* packet did not like to venture through the windings out of the bay, so there we anchored for the night.

* The revolution in Holland had just taken place. The French authorities were dismissed, and on November 26th the Prince of Orange was conveyed from England in H.M.S. *Warrior*. Three days later he landed at Schevening, and on December 1st entered the Hague in state. On December 6th he was proclaimed as William I., King of the Netherlands, laying aside the old title of Stadtholder. General Sir Thomas Graham was appointed to the chief command of the British forces which were despatched to complete the deliverance of the country, and landed off Helvoetsluys, which had been evacuated by the French.

The next morning the wind had changed, and we tossed about till night brought us again to anchor. To-day we proceeded, and luckily met a pilot, who brought us safely in ; if we had not met him we should have had to pass a third night at anchor off [illegible], as our captain had never been here before, and the pilot he has from Harwich has not been here for a great many years.

I shall proceed to-morrow to Rotterdam.

Mr. A. Bradshaw is going to the army till the deputy-paymaster arrives. Roth has found us some lodgings at the commandant's, who is absent, and whose housekeeper has given us rooms and hospitality.

Baron Hempesch is of our party, so far, and I believe he will go to the Hague. This place appears very picturesque by candle-light. I do not know if I shall have time to write to-morrow morning before the packet returns ; if I have, I will. They know no news here.

Letter II.

Saturday.

I have no news to add to-day. We have been walking round the ramparts and courtyard, where there seems a great deal of new artillery. We go to-day only to the Brill, as the carriages are not disembarked.

We have been very comfortably lodged, and are treated with the greatest kindness by the commandant's housekeeper. The weather is remarkably mild ; no symptoms of a Dutch winter.

LETTER III.

The Hague, December 20th, 1813.

ME VOICI ENFIN,

The Dutch ferries are quite as bad as the Scotch, with respect at least to awkwardness in the ferry-men. After being detained above two hours at the Brill with the attempt to boat my carriage, they found that the boat was too small, so I embarked it on board a *schnuyt* and sailed to Haarlem, a very pleasant sail of an hour. As we embarked, the guns at the Brill announced the arrival of the young prince there. He landed at Helvoet very soon after our departure in the morning.

Every house at the Brill was adorned with wreaths of evergreens and flags from all the windows.

From Haarlem, I went to Delft, and my postboy was going through to come on to this place, which is only an hour and a half further ; but it had become dark, and I was uncertain whether I should find lodgings here, and, above all, it was disagreeable to receive undue honours at all the villages, as my carriage was taken for the prince's every-where.

So I stopped at Delft, and saw him pass through in a sort of state carriage, with the burgher guard preceding him, and followed by a crowd singing and huzzaing. All the windows were illuminated.

This morning I came on, and immediately, as soon as I had found a lodging, paid Lord Clancarty* a visit. He was just preparing for the *levée,* and was so good as to send his carriage for me. I am in great luck to have come just in time, as there will not be another *levée* for a week.

* Ambassador to the Hague after the revolution and the accession of the Prince of Orange.

The prince was very civil, inquiring of course after you. So did the young one.

Several other English—a son of Spencer Stanhope's, and a nephew of Mr. Madock's, and others—were afterwards presented, and we were all invited to dine at four o'clock.

The princes are going to make their *entrée* into Leyden to-morrow, when of course there will be a great piece of work, and Lord Clancarty has been kind enough to offer to take me with him. He returns in the evening to make up his despatch, and I shall probably then finish mine. The country is something in the state of England during elections—children singing songs against the French; and how the Landwehr goes on, and how far enthusiasm makes soldiers of them, I do not know, as I have seen very little appearances of military doings.

I have news that Frankfort is no longer the head-quarters, which are changed to Friburg. Bois le Duc is supposed to be taken.

I have not yet had time to hear any detail of news, but before I finish this perhaps I shall be able to give some.

LETTER IV.

The Hague, Tuesday, December 21st, 1813.

Before I tell you about Leyden and to-day, I have in the regular course of things to mention yesterday's dinner, which I thought very agreeable.

To-day I went to Lord Clancarty's at eleven o'clock, and we waited till the princes passed, when we followed their carriages to Leyden, about nine or ten miles off.

Near the town the burgher guard came out, and crowds —the streets as full as possible—shouting and cheering as loud as they could. We went on to the Town Hall at a foot's pace, under triumphal arches, almost squeezing the people to death under the wheels, etc. The dress of the women and Ostade-like countenances of all made it very entertaining.

At the Town Hall the prince received and answered above twenty addresses, which took up about three hours. They then paraded through the streets on foot, and we stuck as close as we could, sometimes nearly all in the canals, as the streets are narrow, and the crowd anxious to see the princes greater than any I ever saw, and on every countenance the greatest signs of joy appeared. After this we returned to the Town Hall, and found an excellent dinner. Clancarty sat by the young prince, and (like Madame de Sevigné's son, you will perhaps think, I agree perfectly with the Duchess of Leeds, and think him extremely agreeable) I really do like him very much, and one cannot help feeling much interested about him.

On the other side (of me) sat M. Kamper, the Rector of the University of Leyden, who is something like Kocloos-key. He is considered a very clever man, and is the author of " The Declaration of the Sovereignty of the Netherlands."

I made an engagement to call on him to-morrow at Leyden, to see the libraries, etc., and he has, I believe, a very good one of his own, and moreover some Aldines (and I believe there are some others to be bought at Leyden); and I am to dine with him, and then I shall proceed to Amsterdam, and return on Friday by Haarlem to *this place*.

We do not hear news here so well as one would expect. About six thousand Dutch soldiers have been raised since the beginning, but one does not see any enlisting or drilling, as I think one ought.

The princesses are coming—the young one to be here

on the 6th of January ; the mother is also *en route* (which I
think they might as well delay).

The communication with Germany seems to be quite
free.   I shall not fix the day of my departure till I return
from Amsterdam.

Lord Yarmouth is backwards and forwards here and at
Rotterdam, etc., trying to buy pictures, but I believe he has
not had much success.

Lord Clancarty is still at an hotel, and impatient to
get a house, as he expects his family.   He is very kind to
me.   Lord Castlereagh * gave me a letter of introduction
to him ; perhaps you will thank him.

LETTER V.

Hanover, Monday, January 3rd, 1814.

Slowly but safely, over execrable roads, and through an
uninteresting country, my journey has lasted six days.   I
wrote a few lines the night before I left the Hague, telling
you that I had seen Amsterdam and Rotterdam.

Mr. Ferrier was in possession of Mr. Crauford's house,
but he had ordered very good lodgings for Lord Bradford
and me at the bath-house on the Boomjees, and he walked
over the town with us.

The next morning we returned to the Hague, as I
believe I before said, and on the 28th I set off.   By-the-
by, at Leyden I bought three Aldines which Lord Clancarty
was so good as to undertake to send to London for me in
three different boxes, directed to me, to be left at Cleveland
House.

I got a route before I left the Hague, from a messenger
who had just arrived from this, and was obliged to make

* Now Secretary for Foreign Affairs in Lord Liverpool's ministry.

détours on account of the French at Deventer. I travelled during the first night, and arrived at twelve next day at Zwolle. I then determined, in consequence of the badness of the roads and parties of Cossacks, of whom I had heard much (but have seen hardly anything), for the future to pass the nights in bed, and have found very comfortable ones.

I came on through Lingen, Osnabruck, Minden, and arrived last night, having performed the journey very comfortably, and am very glad that I have an English carriage.

By sending Behrens on with some of the luggage in a post-waggon I lighten my carriage, and find fires, etc., ready at the inns.

I have seen bad, dirty towns and villages, extensive heaths, sometimes a few fine trees, but nothing one would ever wish to see again.

This town seems to consist of old noggin-houses wretchedly dirty, and very *délabré*. The palace has been by the Westphalians turned into barracks. The Duke of Cambridge * is in one belonging to him.

I called on him this morning, but he was out. I have since met him in the street, and am invited to dine with him.

Colonel Bloomfield and Sir T. Tyrwhitt are here ; the first leaves this on Thursday, and has offered to take anything for me. There is nothing here worth sending.

I shall proceed on Wednesday or Thursday to Cassel.

I believe you had better send any letters for me to the care of *les Frères Schilers* at Berlin. Herries, the banker, will forward them. The head-quarters have been lately at Basle, but they are changing so much that I am still uncertain whether I shall go there. I shall see.

---

* Prince Adolphus Frederick, seventh son of George III., and for some years Viceroy of Hanover.

LETTER VI.

Tuesday evening, January 4th, 1814.

I have just had what I consider great good luck.   On returning from dining with the Duke of Cambridge, with Sir Thomas Tyrwhitt, we found four or five carriages at the door of the inn.   On inquiring, we heard that the Dowager Princess of Orange had just arrived.   Sir Thomas, who had made a great friendship with her at Berlin, instantly announced himself, and, at my desire, told her that I was here, just come from the Hague ; so, of course, I was immediately sent for, introduced to her and her daughter, the Princess of Brunswick, and we stayed with them for a quarter of an hour, till their dinner came, after which they proceeded on their journey.

The Duke of Cambridge has offered me letters for Stuttgart, of which I think I shall avail myself. He has been very kind to me ; for instance, his dinners are provided for him by the States, and he does not invite those whom he is to have to dinner ; but he wrote to the Grand Échanson, Baron de Wengerheim, to desire him to invite me. So I dined yesterday and to-day, and shall to-morrow, after a *chasse de sanglier*, to which I am to go with the said Baron de Wengerheim.

The society is better here than one would expect ; at least, yesterday I was at a very agreeable supper, at a Madame de Dutens', *belle-mère* to Baron de Wengerheim, and to-night there is to be a great assembly at Comte Schweigelt's, at which the duke and all Hanover are to be ; but these, I am told, are the only two houses out of thirty-four that remain belonging to the old noblesse, who were in the habit of living well.

LETTER VII.

Thursday, January 6th.

I have not much to say about the *chasse* yesterday. We left this *en voiture* at six o'clock in the morning, went about ten miles over wretched roads to an inn at the foot of the mountains on the Hamelin road, mounted horses, and rode into the woods, when we were stationed at certain distances with rifle guns' and a little sort of dirk. The weather was very bad, and the dogs found only one or two wild boar, which we had not the good fortune to see. A fox or two was all that was shot.

I had a shot at a deer, and, as usual, missed. The duke had a shot at a fox and missed. We came back very tired and cold, and dined at the duke's at seven.

I am invited to dine with him again to-day, but I am going to take leave and proceed to Cassel, where I hope to arrive to-morrow.

If all the head-quarters are on the other side of the Rhine, as is possible (but this place is so out of the way of news that little is known for certain), I shall probably go from Cassel to Berlin.

If I go further south I shall pay Stuttgart a visit. I must finish now, to be in time for Colonel Bloomfield. Adieu.

I have nothing to say to Char. or Elizabeth,* except that I hope they behave well.

* Lady Elizabeth Gower, the sister of the writer, afterwards Marchioness of Westminster, and still living (1890).

G

LETTER VIII.

Cassel, January 10th, 1814.

Though I have no idea how I shall send a letter from hence, yet, as I have a good opportunity for at least writing, having nothing better to do this evening, I will tell you how I have been amused here, and what I have done.

On my arrival on the evening of the 8th, I sent off a letter Sir T. Tyrwhitt had given me for a M. Badéros (*conseiller privé*, etc.). This occasioned an invitation, before I was up next morning, to dine that day at the Elector's. M. Badéros came soon after, and with him I went and left my name for the Hereditary Prince and Princess (a sister of the King of Prussia). They live in separate houses, and so do the Elector and Electress.

The Hereditary Princess appointed four o'clock for me to be presented to her. I went at half-past one to the Elector's, and found him a gentleman-like enough sort of old man, something in Colonel George Sutherland's way, but younger. His brother, the Landgrave Frederick, told me he had formerly been a great deal in England, and often at my father's house. At dinner, I was placed next to the Countess Hohenstein, who has long been the Elector's favourite—an ugly, coarse person enough. She has been all this time (six years) with him at Prague, the Electress at Gotha.

After dinner, the Elector told me he hoped I should stay some time, and dine every day with him, and that he had ordered a carriage for me to go to his country house, Wilhelmshohe, the next morning; and, accordingly, this morning came my friend M. Badéros, in the Elector's coach and four, like a hackney coach, and took me to see a very fine palace, and a building built by the present Elector in

imitation of the old Gothic castles, with all the old furniture
that he could obtain from all the old castles in the country.
Very well worth seeing and very interesting. And then we
walked over the gardens. Magnificent cascades, and a *jet
d'eau* 190 feet high, extremely grand ; but the morning was
extremely cold and snowy, so much so that a good dinner
and a little of Rhine wine which we ate and drank a little
before one (the Elector's dinner-hour being at half-past
one) did not warm one again. We then came back very
quickly and posted to the dinner. This time the Electress
dined, and the Hereditary Prince and Princess. The
Electress, a vulgar old woman, hoped all our royal family
were well, and ended with desiring to be remembered to
thee.

By-the-by, in the morning M. Badéros, in the course
of our walk, after telling me about the exertions of the
Elector for the good cause, asked me if, as he knew that I
was *très bien avec le* Prince Regent, I could not write to
urge him to assist the Elector with arms and money. I
told him *que je ne pouvais pas me vanter d'être en corre-
spondance*, but that I did not doubt Sir T. Tyrwhitt would
represent everything most favourably. At last he was
contented with my promise that I would recommend the
Elector's case to *monsieur mon père*, for his vote in his
favour, and this he is to tell the Elector I am to endeavour
to obtain.

LETTER IX.

I am to receive the Hereditary Prince and Princess's
letters for Berlin to-morrow morning, and shall proceed
thither by Gotha and Weimar, at both of which courts I
shall remain a day, having got letters of introduction to
their *chambellan's* from hence.

The great head-quarters have entirely broke up, and the armies, having crossed the Rhine, are likely to be soon engaged, which makes it an unseasonable time for visitors in every respect.

By going now to Berlin, and then to Vienna in the spring, we may proceed to the head-quarters south of Germany, Italy, or wherever may be best, so that I have the pleasure of being convinced that I am proceeding most judiciously.

Berlin will not be gay at present, but it will be very interesting to me, and I am sure I shall like it. The Princess of Brunswick and this of Hesse assure me that I shall be well remembered by my friends there.

The only *bore* will be if the Duke of Cumberland * should come there from Strelitz, where I am sorry to say he now is, but I shall take care to find him as little in my way as possible. Adieu.

I had a letter from G. Vernon the day before I left the Hague ; it had come through London. He seems likely to stay at Vienna till Italy opens. Perhaps we may go there together.

LETTER X.

Berlin, Friday, January 20th, 1814.

I arrived here on Tuesday night, without having met with any accidents on the road from Cassel.

I was often detained for horses, and of course found very bad roads ; on this side of Leipsic several bridges destroyed, and one over the Elbe, near Wittenburg, very difficult to descend from on account of some works the French had thrown up.

---

* Ernest Augustus, fifth son of George III., who became King of Hanover on the death of William IV.

I have been received here in the most kind and friendly manner possible by my old Memel friends, quite as much as if they were relations ; but the loss of the queen * has, of course, made a very melancholy difference in the society. I do not believe that ever any person was so much regretted in and out of her family. Her loss is felt as much now as if it had only occurred three months ago.

The Princesses Louise and Guillaume have endeavoured to have as good portraits and likenesses as possible, but I do not think with any satisfactory success. There is a " biscuit" or porcelain bust of her, taken from the mask, and made at the porcelain manufactory for the king. I had desired G. Vernon to procure for me one, but they were not allowed to be sold, so he did what I would not have done, but what I am glad he did—got Princess Guillaume to apply for permission for me to have one, which was given.

The bust ought to have arrived in London scme time ago, but I shall, I hope, discover what has become of it— whether it was intercepted at Hamburgh ; and if it is lost, I shall try to get another ; and if it arrives at Cleveland House,† I shall trust to your taking good care of it, such as having a glass put over it and the box besides. ‡

I shall write further about it. (I have, since writing the above, discovered that it is yet safe here.)

I stayed a day at Gotha to be presented. I was furnished at Cassel with letters to *chambellans*, which is a very good plan, and, indeed, necessary where we have

---

* The beautiful Queen Louise of Prussia, mother of the Emperor William.

† The residence of the Marquis of Stafford, on the site of Bridgewater House.

‡ My father procured many portraits and busts of Queen Louise, and after her lamented death had a marble copy of her monument at Charlottenburg made for him, which is now at Trentham.

no minister.   But, at all events, these letters answer óne's purpose better, for one has only to send it on arriving at night or early in the morning, and an answer comes in half an hour, with an invitation to dine at the palace.

There was nothing very remarkable at that of Gotha— an old, uncomfortable large house.   The duke, a strange-looking sort of likeness of Lord Mountjoy ; the duchess, by whom I sat (in G. Vernon's style), seems a good sort of person.   The next day I proceeded through the town of Erfurth, which had surrendered a few days before, though the citadel still holds out, which made me a little unwilling to go through the town; but after going to Amstadt, several miles round about, I found that, in consequence of the snow, that road to Weimar was not passable, so that through Erfurth I came very safely on to Weimar.   Here I stayed a day, was presented to and dined with the duchess (the duke had arrived at Cassel to take the command of the Hesse troops on the day I left it), the Grand-Duchess Marie, and the Hereditary Prince.   And here I will tell you of a little mistake I have been making, which will perhaps amuse you.

I fancied that the duchess must be the Duchess Louise, of whom Madame de Staël makes such honourable mention in the chapter on Weimar.   Of course, we talked a good deal of the books which they had not received.   I had a copy with me, intended for the Princess Louise here, of which, of course, I made no mention ; but I told the duchess what was said about Weimar, and, on arriving here and finding that the Princess Louise had already a copy, I have sent mine, with a civil note, to the Duchess of Weimar, and have since discovered that the Duchess Louise is the mother of the duke's, and not his wife.   Here my mistake ends, and is, after all, no great joke against me. But I considered her, in consequence, as a person to be extremely respected, which I believe this one deserves too; for she is a person something like the Dowager Duchess of Buccleuch, holding herself very straight and well up, and talking like a very sensible person.

The journey from Leipsic was *triste.* In the first place, all the villages burnt or destroyed, and in the town of Wittenberg, which had, opportunely for me, been taken by storm a few days before, not a house that did not bear marks of war.

The Empress of Russia is daily expected here, on her way to Baden and to the emperor. I have found my Comtesse de Voss in a state of great decadence, having lost her voice and become very deaf, with her memory confused. She was, however, very glad to see me, and took great interest about my lodging, being presented to the Princess Charlotte, the eldest daughter, who is now about fifteen, with a pretty figure, but nothing of her mother's beauty in her countenance.

But the comtesse is in great distress at not being allowed, or able, to do the honours to the empress, whose coming makes a great sensation, as the ladies have not been accustomed to full-dress toilettes, besides being very poor. The sacrifices of all sorts this country has made are not to be described. Not a family that has not lost some relation, and, as an instance of their honourable poverty, at supper at the Minister Goltz's yesterday, the forks were the steel tridents in vulgar use *chez nous.*

All the ladies assist at the hospitals, and contribute all they can for the relief of the wounded and sick, of whom there have been a great number, particularly of old and young who have not been able to support the fatigues. The universal spirit is indescribable.

Sir J. Riddell, who was here about a month ago, wrote a very good letter to his and my friend Inglis (Lord

Sidmouth's private secretary) on the subject of the distress here, and Inglis set up a private subscription and got a few hundred pounds, which was sent here and has been of great use.   If a certain Lord Stafford had not enough to do with his money, and could not say that he had nothing to do with Russia, and could not send assistance to every part of the world that might be in distress, etc., etc., I should take some way or other of hinting to him that he could not do a more charitable thing than to let me sub-scribe something or other for him to these hospitals, etc., etc.; but I do not do it, so don't let me be scolded at. This town, as you have often heard, is beautiful, but I have as yet hardly seen it.

There are no other English here than Mr. King, who has been for six months, in hopes of being somewhere employed.

The King and Queen of Saxony and their daughter are lodged in the palace.   I saw them getting into their carriage yesterday morning, to take an airing, which they do every day, I believe, without having any notice taken of them.

LETTER XI.

27th.

I have in vain been waiting for an opportunity of sending a letter, but as none has occurred this shall take its chance by the post.   The delay gives me an oppor-tunity of telling you that the Empress of Russia stayed here nearly four days.   I took the opportunity of being presented to her, which I had not at Petersburg.   Everybody is delighted with her.   Though she is not handsome, and has a great deal of redness about her complexion, yet she is very pleasing, with much grace and elegance of figure and manners, and extremely civil.

She left this on her birthday. There was a court in the morning, and as she went first to take leave of the Princess Ferdinand, etc., and then dined, and during dinner had a great deal of consultation about the expediency of proceeding on her journey, about which there was a great difference of opinions, on account of the extreme quantity of snow fallen lately, we were kept waiting above four hours to take leave, which was enough almost to do away with the impression we had before conceived in her favour.

I dined at her table the day before, at a very good place for seeing her—nearly opposite. She had an appearance of great melancholy in her countenance, perhaps more so than usually, as she had been in the morning to the monument at Charlottenburg, when they say she was very much affected. The King and Queen and Princess of Saxony paid their court to her, and she paid them a visit; they were also invited to the supper the last evening at the Princess Guillaume's, so that I have also had an opportunity of seeing them.

The princess (for whom I know you feel so much in heart) is a very smiling, good-humoured looking, fat person. They also went to the royal box at the opera, to pay their court to the empress there; and as they were there for some time before she came, and the people falsely imagined that the king had on the order of the Legion of Honour, he was nearly being hooted at. *Au reste*, they are neither insulted nor honoured. I wonder if they will arrive *chez vous*. The Prince Ernest of Mecklenburg is dying or dead. The Duke of Cumberland has been living for some time on the poor Duke of Mecklenburg, who cannot afford to pay for such an honour. Adieu.

LETTER XII.

Strelitz, February 17th, 1814.

The Duke of Cumberland, who has, in all respects, been very civil to me here, has offered to send any letters for me with this to England. You see I profit by every opportunity, and now more readily, as I soon remove to a greater distance, and you will not receive letters so quickly from Vienna, as this is only a day's journey from Berlin, and I wished to see the place and the family. I the day before yesterday put myself *en traineau*, and came in thirteen hours.

The Princess de Solms, whom I had known well at Königsberg, I knew would be glad to see me ; and, accordingly, I began yesterday by breakfasting with her, having first paid my respects to the Duke of Cumberland, who also lives at the *château*. The Duke of Mecklenburg came to see her during breakfast. (And here, in a parenthesis, an account of yesterday will give an idea of the way every day is passed. At ten o'clock the Princess de Solms breakfasts ; the Duke of Cumberland partakes of it, and generally the Hereditary Prince and the Prince Charles, who was severely wounded at, I believe, Leipsic. The Duke of Mecklenburg visits her at the same time, and at half-past two dinner is served ; after which they separate till half-past seven, then reassemble for tea, and at ten supper ; about eleven, take leave and go home.) The duke, who is always spoken of as a very good-natured and excellent man, is, I think, something like George the First, and something like our queen. He has also been very civil, and has pressed me to stay another day more than I intended.

In the evening I was presented to the old Landgrave of

Hesse Darmstadt, whom you have heard mentioned as so respectable a person. There is a constant warfare carried on between her and the Duke of Cumberland, not always in the best taste on his part. *Quant à moi je n'ai que me louer de S. A. R.;* for he lent me four horses this morning to take me in my sledge to Hokenzeritz, a country house of the duke about seven miles off, where the queen* passed her last days, where she went in apparently good health and in the highest spirits at being with her family and at her father's house, with him for whom she had a great affection, and her sister ; and where, in the midst of her joy, she was taken ill, and in a very short time ceased to exist.

Her memory is held as sacred here, and she was so much loved in return by her family, that they have not been able to persuade themselves to live there since.

The king intends, as soon as the materials can be brought from Saxony, which the war has hitherto prevented, to build a temple in the part of the garden which was her favourite spot ; and a sculptor here, of the name of Wolff, has made a very good bust of her, which is to be placed in it.

I have ordered a bust from him. It is much the best likeness I have seen ; indeed, I think excellent.

LETTER XIII.

February 18th, 1814.

This day has been passed in the same way as the other two—a good part of it in talking over the *souvenirs* of Königsberg, and in seeing all those the Princess de Solms has preserved of her sister.

* Queen Louise of Prussia.

I am much pleased with the bust above mentioned. Mine is to be finished in the course of the year, and will be sent to Cleveland House. The face of it is particularly good.

I was delighted to receive your letter of the 21st, the day before I left Berlin. Perhaps I may find another on my return there to-morrow.

I shall, in the course of next week, set off for Vienna, but shall write from Berlin before I go.

I suppose we shall all meet at Paris. All the accounts received lately here are most excellent ; but one never knows if one may believe an account of a victory, etc., till the next brings word how it has been followed up. I am very glad I came here ; it will, at least, afford a subject for conversation for the queen, if she now again should be inclined to honour me so far.

The cold has been uncommonly severe here, as well as with you ; they said to-day at thirteen degrees.

Tell Char. that a lady at Berlin had, this winter, her nose frozen, and in bed while she slept ; her maid first discovered it on calling her, so Char. had better have another blanket.

LETTER XIV.

Berlin, February 26th, 1814, four o'clock.

I am bidding adieu to Berlin, and salute you at the same time ; the carriage is at the door to convey me through Dresden and Prague (at neither of which places I shall stay above a few hours) to Vienna.

I shall probably not stay long there, but perhaps long enough to receive a letter from London. I have been dining at Princess Louise's, and have taken leave of everybody, and end with you. Adieu.

LETTER XV.

Vienna, March 20th, 1814.

I had great pleasure in receiving your letters of the 14th and 16th, which have followed me from Berlin, and arrived together.

You have probably received one from me from Strelitz, and a few lines from Berlin, written just as I was leaving it.

I satisfied myself with a month there, to see everybody there and everything to be there seen (which, indeed, is not much), and am now ready here to take advantage of circumstances.

If I had left England a month sooner (which, however, as you know, I could not well do), I should have been in time for the head-quarters at Frankfort; but as I was too late for that, and did not get to Cassel till the allied armies were in motion across the Rhine, unless I had business there, or intended to serve the campaign, it would not have answered to have followed them; and I do not think I could have taken any better road than I have hitherto done, and I wish I could make up my mind and know what is best to be done next, as I have no wish to remain long here. But before I proceed further in these considerations, I will tell you about my journey, which, however, has been fortunate enough not to furnish any account of adventures or dangers.

I arrived in two days at Dresden, where I stayed one to see the picture-gallery, which has not suffered from the French, as Bonaparte did not take a single picture. The gallery is, I think, almost the only thing worth seeing there. The palace looks shabby, and the town small, with narrow streets. They say the environs are pretty ; but at this season I saw nothing that looked pretty, as far as I could see. After leaving Dresden, I found villages destroyed, and scarcity of houses, and steepish hills on the Bohemian frontier, and a great depth of snow as far as Töplitz, where I was kept a day for want of horses. Here I left the traces of the desolation of war, and what Roth calls fragments of encampments ; but was informed that I should find fevers and illness everywhere, which had spread over the country since the autumn.

These accounts, however, I afterwards found to be exaggerated ; at least, during the extreme cold the mortality at Dresden, etc., has considerably abated, though they are very apprehensive that it will begin again with the spring.

At Prague I stayed a day. A much handsomer town than Dresden ; one part of it on a high hill, on the banks of the Moldau, and very picturesque old churches and tombs, very well worth seeing.

I did not arrive here till the 10th, as nearly to the gates of the town I travelled through snow that had continued to fall, and still continued, and was always up to the axles.

In general the country was uninteresting—some part of it like Hanchurch;* plantations in continued succession, but more of the plain, and everything deep in snow. The towns and villages better than the Westphalian. These are generally white, and the cottages seem comfortable, the inns abominable, and the people seem beasts.

I found George here in very good lodgings, of which I partake. He is, as he had represented himself, in all societies here, which there is no difficulty for anybody to be, whether elegant or not ; but among the *élégantes*, F.

* A village near Trentham.

Lamb is more really at home, without representing himself to be so, and "George is in fact received everywhere" *comme chez vous,* and known as well as among his friends in England. And now I think I have written two lines about him which you may read to the archbishop* or Lady Anne, which they may understand as they like, and you as these are meant; but for you I must add that I heard yesterday that a man who tells people's characters by the shape of their heads said of him, "Mais, mon Dieu, un mulet ne peut pas être plus entêté."

All that your letter contains about the subscriptions for the Berlin hospitals is extremely kind, and I, for them and for me, thank you very much ; all the same, I shall not make you pay for it, as since I wrote there have been sums of money sent from England, and the immediate want and distress was not so great.

I have bought here for you a small box full of the original first Saxon porcelain (called Pekler, or something like it), which is very scarce and consequently curious, and rather pretty. How it will be sent I know not—probably by Trieste to a man-of-war, and may arrive some time or other. I could get more of it at Dresden.

During *Carême* there are no balls here. A little waltzing two nights ago at Comte Palfy's (who was in England some years ago, and is a very good-natured, stupid man) is the only thing of the sort since my arrival. There are several English here—Lord Dumfries, a good-natured sort of little man ; Lord Sunderland, whom I have not yet seen, as he does not go into society, though his tutor does, Mr. Dickenson, of whom you have heard, and who is a very good-natured, extremely silly man, if half the stories they tell of him are true.

---

* Archbishop Vernon Harcourt, of York, who married Lady Anne, sister of the first Duke of Sutherland.

I should wish to get to Rome in time to see it before the summer heat begins, but wish to see a little further what Murat is about.

I am not sure that it would not be a good plan to go from hence to Munich, which is nearer news and more central. I shall, at all events, wait till I receive letters which you will probably have written on receiving my last from Berlin, and perhaps even an answer to this may still be in time for me. At all events, the Comte de Fries, my banker (who has a very fine library, collection of pictures, etc.), will know where to forward it. This must, I believe, trust itself to the post, perhaps through France.

I wish the conferences were over, and that the allies had a very good general; for Blucher, who has done the best, though a very brave and active hussar, is very old, and nobody, even here, mentions with praise, *on n'est pas si bien pensant ici quâ Berlin.* If you cannot read this letter you may suppose that it is badly written on purpose to prevent its being read everywhere on the road. Thanks to C. L. Gower and E. M. L. Gower for their letters.

LETTER XVI.

Vienna, April 17, 1814.

I am now very glad to have waited here for the crisis to which things have so happily come in France, on which I need not expatiate from hence, but be content with rejoicing.*

I think it possible we may see something of one another in the course of the summer, but in a few weeks we shall be better able to judge. Your letters of the 7th and 8th gave me much pleasure, though they were a long time on

* The (temporary) restoration of the Bourbons.

the road; not so long, however, as your post of the 27th of December, of which, I believe, Lord Castlereagh had been the bearer, and which arrived here about a fortnight ago. You have, of course, heard of Madame de Vessenburgh, of her having been taken by the French peasants, and at last liberated by Bonaparte, after long conversations. We were for some time very uneasy at the accounts from France, till the last affairs and taking of Paris set all up again.

There has been no court here since I came, and, consequently, no opportunity of being presented to the empress. But a Baron de Sichengen, a great friend of the emperor and empress, showed me one day her apartments, and we contrived to meet her on the way, which was almost as good. You would be entertained at hearing of some of the parties we have given, such as dinners to the Prince de Ligne and Princess Chimay, and to the Princess Maréchale de Lubomirska, a sister to the old Prince Czartorisky, and an extraordinary old lady in the Dowager Essex way.

Yesterday *I* gave a very pleasant breakfast at Laxenburg, a country house of the emperor, about fourteen or fifteen miles off (the breakfast, though, was at the inn), to the Ligne and Lubomirska's family; and we had a very pleasant day. Among the other things to be seen is a small new-old castle, filled with real old and very curious furniture—relics from old abbeys and castles, such as beds of Charles V. and Rudolf II., armour of Maximilian, old pictures, tapestry, etc. You would, all of you, have enjoyed it very much. The old Princess Maréchale, above mentioned, has the prettiest house in Vienna—almost the only one that is well and comfortably furnished.

I saw Madame de Mervelt (?) this morning, and told her all you said of her, which gave her great pleasure. She

H

means to set off soon, but is in difficulties and uncertainty about the most advisable road, etc.

The Starembergs have been very civil. She wishes to be remembered to you ; so does the poor old Comte de St. Prie, who has not yet been informed of the death of his son, who is much regretted. He was wounded at Kleins (?), and died after suffering very much for some time.

It is very melancholy to see the old man still uncertain and in hope, though the death is known by everybody else, and will, I suppose, be so to him to-morrow.

George Vernon is very anxious to know what account I gave of him, but I shall content myself with what I before said, except that *I think* he will be better for his travels.

I do not know where to be directed to at Paris (how odd it sounds !), but I should think under cover to Lord Abercrombie would be the safest way.   Adieu.

LETTER XVII.

Vienna, April 19, 1814.

Just as we are in the act of putting the last hand to packing up, to set off to France, Nott brings me in your letter of the 17th ult., to my great joy.

I cannot comply with the order contained in the last line, to write long letters and in detail, at this moment, because Lamb's servant, who has brought the letter, says the messenger is going off immediately ; but I will write again from Munich. I wrote a letter to you the day before yesterday.

Every courier brings better and better news from France. It is very likely we did not go to Italy in too great a hurry.

Loch's letter of attorney must be sent to Paris. Who

knows but that I may pay you a visit in the course of the summer, or you me one at Paris?

I could never have thought it possible for Bonaparte to end so wretchedly.

Madame de Mervelt means to set out on the 26th, but will probably be a long time on the road. She is to determine her route from the accounts we may send her at Munich. Adieu.

For Paris, hurrah!

LETTER XVIII.

Stuttgart, April 28th, 1814.

So far so well. On our way to Paris we stayed a day or two at Munich. Were presented to the King and Queen of Bavaria, which is not much of a court. We saw the picture-gallery, which is, I believe, now the next finest to Dresden.

Munich is a moderate sort of a town, in a plain, ugly enough sort of country. But I cannot say enough in praise of the country of Salzburg, which is quite beautiful.

The road from Lintz to Salzburg is in sight of very fine distant mountains, with snowy tops. All the nearer hills are covered with various wood—spruce firs, forest trees, and fruit trees, and the valleys and plains are well culti-vated; and altogether it offers an appearance of a mixture of park, farm, and garden, which is delightful.

The town of Salzburg is surrounded by fine mountains, and is very picturesque. We were sorry to pass so quickly through such a country, though the good road and good horses make a contrast with the parts of Germany I had before seen, which is not unpleasant when one has a long journey before one.

For Bavaria—at least, all between Vasserburg on the Inn and Ulm—I cannot say much. This of Wirtemberg is much better ; hills covered with vines and fruit trees in abundance, thriving in a rich soil and water meadows.

The court are at Ludwigsburg, a few miles off. We have seen the palace this morning, which is magnificent. An innumerable number of rooms fitted with rich and handsome furniture, immense stables, and altogether a most kingly establishment. But all this magnificence is said to be dearly paid for by the country, and the government so bad and tyrannical that it cannot long be endured.

The late events in France have had corresponding effects in Italy. The King of Bavaria had a letter from the viceroy, informing him that he had resigned himself to the Emperor of Austria, and requesting his father-in-law's good offices.

I hope Murat will soon be ousted.

It will be very interesting at Paris to see how the constitution and all will go on. We shall go there through Strasbourg, and my next letter will be dated from Paris. I should be obliged to you to send me Brougham's "Appeal to the Allied Nations in behalf of Poland" by any good opportunity, of which, I suppose, there will be no scarcity.

Have you received any of my letters from Vienna ? A small box of old original Dresden china, which I mentioned in one, was sent to Trieste, with some boxes of Captain Cadogan's, to be taken charge of by Captain Gower, so that it may be some time before you receive it.

You seem to have had more waltzing in London than we have in Vienna—at least, since I came there. All that we had was once or twice at Count Palfy's, who was in England some years ago, and is a good-natured, stupid German.

Starhemberg * set off for Paris by courier of a sudden, without saying a word to anybody, to endeavour, I believe, to get appointed ambassador there. His circumstances are said to be worse than those of any of the great Austrian nobles, who all seem in bad circumstances.

Vernon fancies himself very sorry at leaving Vienna— very unnecessarily.

LETTER XIX.

Paris, May 4th, 1814.

Though we have not yet been here long enough to give a settled, detailed account of things, you may think it worth while to hear that we have arrived safe.

I wrote a few lines at Stuttgart, but found that the best thing to do with them was to bring them on to this, when they are at your service.

We arrived the night before last, and, after a long search, have found a miserable lodging in a garret of the Hôtel d'Arboit, Rue Traversière, St. Honoré.

The swarms of English, etc., etc., etc., have filled the town to a degree unparalleled.

The king † and the Duchess d'Angoulême made their entry yesterday, went to Notre Dame, and, preceded and escorted by the National Guards, to the Tuileries. A great mob, of course, but not the enthusiasm one hears of at London.

In the evening, illuminations, crowds in the Tuileries, and the king appeared for a short time at a window. A good deal of shouting.

* Austrian ambassador at the court of St. James in 1807.

† Louis XVIII., after the signing of the treaty of abdication between the Emperor Napoleon and the allied powers, had started on his progress from London to Paris, and touched French soil on April 25th. Thence he proceeded by Compiègne and St. Ouen to the capital.

This morning the foreign troops paraded before him at his window, and it was a magnificent sight to see them —the finest men and horses possible—all looking fresh and healthy, and fit for victories.

It was a grand triumphal spectacle. One cannot get over one's wonder and admiration of all one sees.

LETTER XX.

May 5th.

Sir Charles Stuart * gave a great ball last night, at which were Lord Wellington, Blucher, Platoff, Ney, Beresford, etc., etc., etc., of all nations and classes ; emperor, princes, generals, and all the English faces one sees at every London ball.

Mackenzie, who has offered to take this, will, I dare say, be happy to give an account of it.

I walked in the morning to take a look at our old house, and found over the door, "Hôtel du Maréchal Prince d'Eck Mühl." The garden and outside look much the same as formerly, and Madame de Coigny, whom I saw yesterday, and who desires her compliments, says that the inside is very well furnished.

I believe the Grand-Duke Constantine is in possession.

I have heard from everybody about you so lately that I almost feel as if I had seen you.

If you want any advice from me about coming here, I believe I would advise you to wait a little, as everything is in great confusion ; no lodging to be had, and I hear that, as one might expect, no society yet, except Lord Castlereagh's suppers to *vingtaines* of the English.

* Ambassador at the court of France, afterwards created Lord Stuart de Rothesay.

The improvements since our time are said to be very great. Now we are so near, I shall write very often, perhaps to Char. and Eliz. In the mean time I trust to Mackenzie to make my excuses to them, and refer them to him for any information they may require, but I must not keep him waiting. Adieu.

The Duc de Berri * was very glad to see me yesterday. I hallooed out in the crowd the other morning, "Vive, Monsieur!" as loud as I could as he passed, but he did not hear.

LETTER XXI.

Paris, Saturday night, May 14th, 1814.

Wilmot was to have gone to London two days ago, and I wrote, in a great hurry, a letter for him to take, when he postponed his departure, and I could not send my letter by the common post, as it is said to be extremely uncertain. Now he is again to go to-morrow, and will, I hope, take this safely, to let you know that Lord Ilchester has this evening given me your letter, which it gave me much pleasure to receive.

What the *malveillants* in London say about France has, I fear, too much foundation. There appears to be a great deal of discontent.

They complain of the protracted stay of the allied troops ; and, to be sure, no one can conceive nothing more galling for the French people than to have Russian *patroles* in their streets and at their barriers, etc.

Many duels have taken place among the officers, and some fighting occasionally among the men. This was to

* Son of the Comte d'Artois, afterwards Charles X., and grandfather of the Comte de Chambord.

be expected; but, besides, there appears to be very little enthusiasm for the Bourbons.

The soldiers regret Bonaparte, which one would not have expected ; but it is everywhere the case.

The discontented murmur at the terms of peace. Yesterday a petition was presented by some hundreds of workmen to the king, complaining of want of employment; and the reduction of the army will, of course, occasion an increase of number of idle hands, and there will be a great want of money to carry on affairs.

Everybody is astonished at the publication of the intention to reduce the French navy to thirteen ships, and, as Lord Castlereagh declares that this is not in consequence of any demand of his, it does seem a very ill-timed and unnecessary declaration ; in short, between the allies and the French, the king will have a very bad time of it.

I went to Monsieur's * levée a few days ago ; he came up immediately to me, and shook hands, and asked after you, and desired to be remembered, all very kindly.

I am invited to dine at the Prince de Condé's to-morrow, at the petit Palais Bourbon.

The Corps Législatif (as you know) have occupied the Palais Bourbon, with a new portico, etc., and the Hôtel de Brienne had been destined for the reception of the prince ; but he said he preferred his own house, and accordingly drove at once to the petit Palais, and is, as fast as he can, turning the Corps Législatif out of doors.

I went with Lord Bradford yesterday to see Malmaison. After walking over the gardens we saw a M. de Beaumont, formerly chamberlain to the Empress Josephine, to whom Lord Bradford had procured a letter of introduction to have leave to see the house ; and while we were with him, the

* The Comte d'Artois, afterwards Charles X.

empress, hearing of our being there, came into the room
and invited us to her drawing-room to sit down, and talked
very well, with very good manners and good taste, for some
time ; invited us to breakfast on Monday to see her son,
the Prince Eugène, who arrived a few days ago, and has
been very well received by the king, to whom he said that,
though he was still much attached to the person of Bonaparte, he trusted that he might still be a faithful subject of
his Majesty.

Everybody praises his conduct very much in all respects.

She (Josephine) has been very civil to the English.

I think the breakfast will be entertaining. The day
before yesterday, I went to the Luxembourg to see M.
Cuvier and the Jardin des Plantes. There is enough in
Paris to see for many mornings, and good plays in the
evening.

To-day I have seen the Luxembourg, St. Geneviève,
and, among other persons, Madame de Vaudemont ; she
has desired me to say many things to you—how much she
longs to see you, means to write, fears you will not care,
etc., etc.

Madame de Staël is arrived ; I have not seen her yet,
but I hear she has begun to give her opinions very freely
in praise of English and abuse of French.

If you want some very handsome boole (certainly
wrong spelt) furniture, bookcases, or Indian screens, you
have only to tell me, and I can procure them, Lord Kin-
naird says, very cheap, though Fogg has bought up an
immense quantity of things to sell immensely dear.

P.S.—The Duc de Bourbon, at dinner, drank your
health, and sent many compliments to you.

LETTER XXII.

Paris, May 23rd, 1814.

Since I wrote by Wilmot, I have received from Vienna
your two letters of the 29th March and 12th April, and
the Polish pamphlet of the 17th, and this morning the joint
one from you and the children of the 19th, for all of which
many thanks.

The dinner at the Palais Bourbon (at which Clive,
who is to take this, dined) was entertaining enough.
Two of the *maréchaux* dined, Marmont and Moncey, and
the Prince de Conde, during dinner, annoyed the first by
asking him if he had been at Paris before the Revolution.
"Oh oui, monseigneur, souvent." "Et à la cour?"
"Monseigneur, j'était trop jeune."

Lord Bradford and I went to the breakfast at Malmaison, to which I told you we were invited, and which we
found in all respects a good dinner, at half-past eleven
o'clock. Champagne, Burgundy, etc., and regular courses.

She afterwards took us into the gallery to show pictures
and statues, and invited us to dinner for two days after.

At dinner we found the Grand-Duchess of Baden ; the
Prince Royal of Bavaria, of whom we heard at Munich
as a man of abilities, but his manners do not indicate as
much. You will see in England what a quiz he is. He
has taught himself English, and on seeing our red uniforms,
he came across a sort of circle before dinner to Lord
Bradford, and in a very loud tone of voice—for he is
very deaf—accosted him with, "What is your name, sir?"
"Lord Bradford, sir." "And that name?" pointing to
me ; and then to me, "Your lordship is very young!"
"Pretty well, sir." "About twenty?" "Near twenty-
eight, sir." "Ah, that is near my own age."

I do not think this seems so entertaining on reading it, but it seemed very much so to us at the time.

He then said to Lord Bradford, "Are you a gambler, sir?"

The Queen Hortense,* who seemed an agreeable person but very consumptive, and the Prince Eugène also dined. After dinner we had some music; Josephine's manners are certainly very good.

She is short, and seems growing fat and something like Mascale in the face. To wander from her, I will proceed to the Duchess d'Angoulême, to whom I have been this morning. On my name being given, she said, "Oh, je connais Lord Gower fort bien," inquired after you, and spoke for a few minutes to me, and then proceeded with other presentations, which she seemed to do very well, as far as I saw, which extended to four or five French generals.

Now I will proceed further, and, as I am so near May 29th, I will pay you a visit in a fortnight hence. I intend to let the emperor, etc., go their ways first, and shall come after (not caring for the great fêtes, etc.), and arrive *chez vous* about June 6th, and then purpose, about ten days after, to take a start to Dunrobin (with Elizabeth, of course), and then back to you at Trentham, and then through this again to Switzerland, etc.

I have been dining with a numerous party at Lord Castlereagh's; among others, the Sovereign Prince of Orange, who arrived, accompanied by Lord Clancarty, suddenly yesterday.

The Emperor of Russia, they say, won't go in a man-of-war, but in a packet. I wish his humility might find

* Queen Hortense (the wife of Louis Bonaparte, King of Holland, and mother of Napoleon III.) and Eugène Beauharnais were the children of Josephine by her first marriage.

reason to be contented in England, and that people would take no notice of him.

They also say that he is insisting with Louis XVIII. on having Caulincourt as ambassador at Petersburg, and that the king perseveres in refusing.

The young Prussian princes are not sure yet if they are to go with their father or not.

Who should I see in the Louvre this morning but G. Bishton ? Lord Forbes will take this, as he goes first.

Clive will, perhaps, have another for to-morrow evening, a duplicate, to cause Elizabeth the trouble of copying. Madame de Vaudemont also dined to-day at Lord Castlereagh's. She is an old friend of his. Lady Castlereagh has the most admirable ignorance of persons that can be conceived ; all foreigners are foreigners to her.

LETTER XXIII.

Paris, June 2nd, 1814.

Poor Empress Josephine's death was very sudden, after a very short illness, of a putrid sore throat.

Lady Castlereagh drove there to see her (she had heard the night before of her not being well), and was told that she had died in the morning. The day before, the Empress of Russia dined there. She was then obliged to stay in her own room. Her son and daughter dined, and they had no idea of her danger.

END OF PART II.

PART III.

PART FIVE

LETTER I.

Paris, September 30th, 1816.

As Wilmot, who has been with Ward till this time, goes to England to-morrow, I take the opportunity of saying that I am safe and well so far. I arrived the day before yesterday, and proceed to-morrow. I had a very good passage of four hours, and a prosperous journey— good weather. I have seen nobody here but some English Talbots, who are to be home by the middle of October. She likes Paris very much. Several others are here, but none very interesting to write about. I have also made the acquaintance of Dr. Denon, to whom Littleton had sent a letter by me.

I was delighted with his apartments; some good pictures, many bronzes, antique, and copies of the antique from Herculaneum, all arranged with much taste, and he very civil.

I am sorry, selfishly as well as humanely, to hear that the Burghershes * are in great sorrow at the loss of their child, and are on their way home, so that a good house for visiting at Florence is lost.

It may be stupid to have no news to send from hence, but I have none, so I shall say good-bye, and dress to dine at Verey's, *et puis au Théâtre Français.*

---

* Lord Burghersh was afterwards known as Lord Westmoreland, who was British ambassador in Berlin, Vienna, and Florence.

I went yesterday to Versailles to see the waters play. Very gay; the gardens full of people, and *Lady Binning* there.

Travelling makes me inclined to be expensive in great things and stingy in common—penny wise and pound foolish; but I mean to be very prudent. Adieu.

LETTER II.

Geneva, October 7th, 1816.

The post-horses between Paris and this place have been so much knocked up by the numbers of travellers, that I did not reach this till yesterday morning. I slept the night before at Gex, one stage off, because the gates here are shut at an early hour, and came on early in the morning.

I drove over to pay Madame de Staël a visit at Copet, and found, to my great surprise, the Vernons * sitting on each side of her, paying a morning visit. They have been staying here for a month, for her to bathe in the cold bath here, and to receive letters from Lord Lucan about going to Italy, which the total failure of receipt of rents makes uncertain for him.

They, however, set off on Thursday, and take with them her sister, Lady Louisa, whose marriage with Mr. Stewart is off, on account of some outrageous propositions on his part with regard to settlements.

I shall not travel over the Simplon with them, though, but continue in company with a Mr. Nariskie, with whom

* The Vernons were the son and daughter-in-law of the Archbishop of York, who was married to Lady Anne Gower, the aunt of the writer, and who on succeeding to the Harcourt estates assumed that name. Mr. Vernon's wife was a daughter of Lord Lucan. Her sister became eventually the Countess of Wemyss.

I fell in half-way from Paris hither, and with whom I shall go on to Milan, more for security than society, as two carriages of men are stronger than one, and there have been robberies lately.

It is supposed that the Hopes were the object of a party of robbers, who, by mistake, robbed Mr. Lister of Shropshire of all he had, and wounded Mr. Hope's courier, who rode up at the time, and endeavoured to return to warn the Hopes. They stayed for a little while at the stage before and escaped. Since that, one or more of the robbers has been taken and executed, and Jerseys, and Cowpers, and Dr. Dunganville, and others have passed in safety.

The Duchess de Broglie * is not improved in beauty by her marriage, but looking very dirty. She and Madame de Staël go to Paris in ten days. I have had very fine weather. The harvest is excessively late everywhere, and I have seen fields of oats still uncut, as far as on this side of Gex.

I met on the road Prince Kazaloosky, going to Paris for three months, to put himself *au fait* of the real state of things ; he is to make Turin as agreeable to me, on my return, as he can.

I have hired a *voiturier* to take me to Milan, to set off the day after to-morrow, and to arrive there on the sixth day.

Vernon wrote a long letter to me some time ago, giving an account of the breaking off of the marriage, which, if you should receive, you are authorized to read.

Bread is very dear here, and good bread very scarce, and the poorer people likely to suffer much distress. Adieu.

* Daughter of Madame de Staël.

I

8th, at night.

We go off early to-morrow morning. Just come from dining at Vernon's, and shut out. Luckily a Génevois—I suppose one of the *petit* council—was in the same case and had sent to the syndic, who had gone to bed (at eleven o'clock), and we got in under his wing. *Le plus beau temps du monde.*

LETTER III.

Milan, October 16th, 1816.

I begin as usual by saying that I arrived safe and well here, the day before yesterday. We had most delightful weather for the journey, and the passage over the Simplon did not disappoint my expectations. The rocks and mountains, among which the road is made, especially on the south side, are as grand and sublime as possible, and the road is wonderfully engineered and well made, that one is delighted and astonished the whole way. It is not suffered to go to decay, as the Valois employ a certain number of workmen—they said a hundred and fifty, but I did not see above thirty or forty—in repairing their share of it; and on the Sardinian part it is still in perfect repair, though the stone posts, which are put up at every two yards on the precipice road, seem to have been pushed by some mischievous persons, in imitation of the Highland way of throwing down parapets. So much for that. Of course one cannot pass the Simplon without saying something about it, though one has already heard so much about it that it may be enough to say that one has not been disappointed with it.

We met with no robbers or misadventures. I go to-morrow to Genoa, whence I shall return hither to go to

Como, Bergamo, Brescia, etc., etc., to Venice, and to touring in a way to see as many of the towns of the north as possible—on to Florence. I take leave of my Russian companion, who did very well for the high-road, but not so well for cultivated Italy. *Je ne me suis pas encore accoutumé* to the pleasure one feels at being in Italy. I am going this morning to Monza to see the palace, iron crown, etc., and shall finish this in the evening, as I hear the post goes at that time.

LETTER IV.

October 17th.

I have nothing to add, except that I believe that the rains are setting in, which will be a disagreeable affair, but necessary and to be expected.

I am just going off to Genoa, with Lady William Bentinck's letters, in a light carriage, which I have hired here for the purpose. I shall write from hence on my return in a week.

The Princess of Wales * left this place a short time ago ; at Monza they said she was expected there to-day.

She is, I believe, building near the Lac Como. I have bought a few very fine Aldines, but none of very much consequence.

Write to Florence, to the bankers, Mess. Donato Orsi, as I shall probably not stay above a day or two at Vienna or at any other place on my way. Adieu.

The post that went yesterday goes through Holland ; this is to go through France to-morrow morning. I wrote from Geneva.

* Afterwards Queen Caroline. The details of her life near Lake Como were often referred to during her trial before the House of Lords.

LETTER V.

Verona, October 28th, 1816.

I have not written to you since I left Milan for Genoa, a journey which required two days, the road over the Borchetta extremely bad and jolting. I stayed three days at Genoa. Lady William Bentinck's friends, to whom she had given me letters, were unfortunately out of town, *villégiaturing*. However, I saw everything remarkable there. I was rather disappointed with regard to beauty of architecture, but the *palazzi* are certainly very large and fine, and there are still some good pictures to be seen. I sailed out a little way to see the town from the sea, and along the coast for seven miles, when I landed at Pegli and walked back, seeing some gardens and *palazzi* on the way. Lord and Lady Ponsonby have been there for some months, and pass the winter there, which is a terrible *ennui* for her.

I returned to Milan, and the day after my return set out with the Vernons for Bergamo, which is most delightfully situated at the foot of the Alps; but first I forgot to say that in returning from Genoa I met swarms of peasants, old men and children, on the road. I was informed at Casteggio that some thousands had passed within three or four days from Parma and Piacenza, emigrating to Spain, and that it appeared that there was some mistake or bad intention on the part of those who had encouraged their emigrating, as these people went under the idea of finding at Genoa means for transporting them to Spain; but that several had already returned disappointed, the Spanish consul at Genoa having heard nothing about them from his Government. These wretched people, having disposed of their houses at home, were returning in despair and starving. They are subjects of Marie Louise, whose Government does not seem popular. Indeed, there seems considerable discontent with the Governments wherever I have been—at Genoa, and in the Milanese and Venetia.

Letter VI.

Venice, October 31st.

We arrived here the day before yesterday. We had a very pleasant journey, first day to Bergamo, second to Brescia, third to Verona, where we stayed a whole day, and where I wrote the first sheet of this, which was interrupted by our going to see some feats of horsemanship (like Astley's) in the amphitheatre, which we had seen empty in the morning. As it was a Sunday, and the troop of equestrians had only entered that morning, there was a considerable crowd—they said about three thousand. A sufficient extent of the amphitheatre was filled in one part from bottom to top, to give a good idea of its appearance when full, and one felt as if one had seen it in its former time.

We slept at Padua the next day after seeing Vicenza, and thence came here. We had fine October weather during our journey ; since we arrived here it has been rainy and siroccoish. However, we have seen the Doge's palace, etc., and in it many magnificent pictures. Eugène * contrived to prevent the French from taking many pictures, and most that were taken have been restored. I believe you have both been here, so that I need not expatiate on the subject, but there is more appearance of decadence since then ; at least, in wet weather it looks very *triste* and dripping. I shall stay four or five days. I believe we

* Eugène Beauharnais was created by Napoleon Viceroy of Italy.

shall separate here.   The Vernons go to join their child at
Bologna, and I shall make a start for Mantua, and thence
an acute angle to Bologna.   I shall stay a day at Padua on
my return, as we did not half see it, and one can see places
better by one's self than with women dragging after.   Lady
E—— and her sisters are both very good-natured and good
travellers, but I shall, for variety, like very well to go alone
again, till I fall in with somebody else.   I have hitherto
found travelling in Italy extremely good—excellent roads.
I shall leave this on Monday, November 4th.   Adieu.

LETTER VII.

Novi, November 7th, 1816.

I wrote from Venice, which we left on Monday last, the
4th, and were not sorry to leave it, as it is a disagreeable
place enough, especially in wet weather, which was the case
with us the greater part of the time.   We parted at Padua.
The Vernons took the Verona road to Mantua, as the
straight road through Ferrara to Bologna, which they had
intended to take, was described as nearly impassable from
the deep mud about Ferrara; and I came by Este and
Legnago.   About eight miles from Padua, I stopped to
see the old castle of V. Obizzi, which Eustace describes
as well worth seeing, and I was very much pleased
with it.   It belongs now to the Duke of Modena, to whom
it was left about fourteen years ago, by the last of the
Obizzi family.   I drove from Mont Sta. Elena to Arqua to
see Petrarch's house and tomb.   The house is very pleasantly
situated, with some old paintings in fresco as a broad
fringe round two or three rooms.   They show an old chair
and bookcase and an inkstand of his.

It was a rainy day, but I was determined to see these

places, and was not disappointed with them, and my conscience is satisfied.

At Mantua I saw the palaces of the Gonzagas.   The old one is becoming a ruin, but has still remains of magnificence of Giulio Romano and Mantegna; the new one, joining the other (pretty old, too), is very large—much of it painted by Giulio's scholars, and it contains the tapestry from some of Raphael's cartoons.

The Palazzo del Tè, which is, however, square, has suffered from war and weather, but is still curious, from all that remains of Giulio Romano in it.

I have been stopped here on my way to Modena for want of horses, and shall remain at Modena to-morrow and the next day.   I shall overtake the Vernons at Bologna, when I shall leave them to make their way to Rome and take mine to Florence, without wife or child to carry.

Letter VIII.

Modena, November 8th.

A poor place enough, and I did not content myself with seeing the palace, where there are some good pictures, and go on to Bologna, as there is no opera or play to-night, because it is, I don't know what, Friday.   I shall take my letter on to Bologna, as the post had gone from hence before my arrival, and I shall be in time for the next at Bologna.

I arrived this morning, the 9th, in time to breakfast with the Vernons.   I left Modena at five to get the start of all the English, who were numerous, as horses are few on the road, and inns full.

There is more to see here than I expected, and I shall remain to-morrow.

I have nothing particular to say of the weather here. Not much Italian sky to boast of; the rainy season, I suppose, not quite over, as there has been some on most days lately; however, good weather on the whole for November. I begin to be impatient to hear from you, which I shall do at Florence. In my next letter from thence I shall say what I know about my further proceedings.

I think I shall probably stay about three weeks there, and a week for Lucca, Pisa, Leghorn, and so be at Rome in about a month. Adieu.

LETTER IX.

Florence, November 18th, 1816.

I have provided myself with some bad, thin writing paper of this place, that my letters may not be over-weight and dear. I like Florence very much; it would be better if it were less full of English. At the only two houses I have been, the Countess d'Albany's and Madame Hitroff's, it was like a bad English crowd, where one knew very few people; those one did know were such as Lady Breadalbane, Lady Liddell, and, except Jerseys and Cowpers, very few one would care to see. But there is a great deal to see in the way of fine arts, and it is a clean town, and, though very cold and sharp frost, weather not unpleasant for going about. I have been to-day over Fiesole, which was delightful. I have been twice to the Palais Pitti, which is, as I suppose it was formerly, full of good pictures—eight Raphaels among others. I have not half seen the gallery yet. In short, I shall have enough to keep me a good fortnight here, besides an excursion to Lucca, Pisa, and Leghorn, though it is not quite the right season.

From society here I do not expect much, but the Jerseys and Cowpers are very agreeable in the way of dinners. The Fitzherberts pass the winter here, though they neither seem to like it much. Baron Trippi has put a tragical termination to his life here, a few days before I came here. Mrs. Fitzherbert is supposed to have been somehow partly the cause, but I think pecuniary distress a more probable one. I have not heard much about it. The Lawleys are also passing the winter here, and your friends the Liddells. I have not received any letter from you yet; I yesterday received one from Char. of the 6th of October, enclosed in one from Lady William Bentinck of the 29th; but the chief contents of the packet were, unfortunately, a large letter from G. Vernon from Switzerland, and one from Mr. Arbuthnot, informing me of the name of a Mr. *Gervas Cole Brown* having been inserted in the list transmitted to the Excise, in order to his being instructed in the duty of an officer of that revenue. Of this I should be obliged *to you to inform the Dean of Lichfield*, as I applied at his request; and pray thank Char. for her letter. I am glad to find she took possession of my house so soon, and hope she will again as often as she or Surrey may find it convenient. I had a good deal of snow in crossing the Apennines. We were all much struck with a picture at Bologna, in the Aldobrandini Palace, a portrait by Pamigiano.* Talking of pictures the other day here, I asked the Cowpers if they had seen it, when they said they had been equally pleased with it, and that it was for sale, and only 400 sequins, or £200, asked for it, and Lord Cowper quite sorry at the time that he could not buy it, and that nobody did. As they ask £200, they would probably take £150. I can inquire further on my return, if wished.

* This portrait of a handsome youth is now in the Stafford House gallery.

Please to direct your next letter to me to Rome, *aux soins du Duc de Torlonia.* I am sorry to hear of Belvoir's misfortune.

Madame Apponyi, whom Lady William Bentinck described as such an agreeable person, is unfortunately not here; her other letters have been very well received. I intended to have written to the Duchess of Cumberland by this post, but shall not. If you have any communication, will you say that she is threatened with one soon from hence; that I have been waiting for some opportunity of sending a letter, but that none except the post offers itself? Prince Henry of Prussia, the king's eldest brother, is here, and going to Rome to see the world.

The Fitzherberts have seen no place in their travels half so pretty as Trentham.

This town is so full of English that I had difficulty in getting lodgings, and was for four days in very bad, but am now very well off. I have written to Vernon to secure some for me against the 14th or 15th of next month at Rome. Addio.

What account from Scotland? So cold here I can hardly write.

I will for the future number my letters to you ; the last I wrote from Bologna.

LETTER X.

Florence, November 24th, 1816.

I was delighted to receive yesterday your letter of the 2nd. In answer to the last part of it, about the Duchess of Devonshire's letter in the newspaper, giving a bad account of robberies in Italy, I have not heard of any excepting those I mentioned in Lombardy, and if there were many one would certainly hear more of them, when the roads are covered with English travellers ; and I don't mean to travel in the dark.

The Campbells are just arrived here. The Jerseys go to Rome to-morrow. The Cowpers have been much plagued with the illness of a servant, occasioned, it is supposed, by his eating too many oysters at Venice, where they are found on poisonous copperous rocks. They were detained for a week at Bologna, and obliged to leave him at one post on this side of it on their way, and the poor man has died there.

I shall set out on the 28th for Lucca, etc., and return about the 5th here, and stay a day or two on the way to Rome. I shall write from hence on my return. I have bought a few little bronzes here, and some books.

I learn here that the green marble or stone which is at Trentham put in the front of the stands for your Assynt marble in the hall is serpentine, and I think they call that which is in the dining-room at Cleveland House, near the shut-up window, marble of Genoa.

The court has been for some time at Pisa, but I believe it makes very little difference where it is. The very cold weather has changed to warmer—very rainy.

This is as good a place to be at, in fact, as any I know of. I suppose Rome will be as good. One ought certainly to see this place in the spring, as Valombrossa, etc., are at present inaccessible ; but I think I shall persevere in my intention of returning by the Ancona road, especially if the weather permits me to go to Pisa, etc., now. There is an excellent bust-maker here, Bertolini, but as you have one already of me, I have not thought it advisable to repeat the likeness ; he has done one of Mrs. Middleton and of Mrs. Foley, whom one has seen about in London—two great guys, which are so like that everybody is amused with them.

The French had taken nothing from the gallery here. The Venus which belongs to it, and is now restored to it, had fallen into their hands elsewhere, but I don't believe they disturbed the gallery in the least. From the Palais Pitti they had taken a great many pictures, which have all come back. The Venus looks much better here than at Paris. This place does not swarm with beggars like the rest of Italy; they are shut up in a former convent and obliged to work, which was the case at Venice, till the Austrians sent them all out to starve.

Tuesday, 26th.

Post-day. I have not much to add. My love to all concerned. Adieu.

LETTER XI.

Florence, Friday evening, December 5th, 1816.

I returned hither this evening, after a most delightful excursion of nine days. The first I saw the villa of Poggio, Cojàno, Prato, Pistoja; the second to Lucca; the third to Massa and Carrara, to see the quarries, which being about two miles from Carrara is a *paese fiero* indeed, and a much worse road from there to Carrara. The Queen of Etruria not having taken possession of Lucca, the Austrians have done so, and levy taxes on the people such as they never knew of before. It is a delightful country. The fourth day to Pisa, where I was enraptured with the Campo Santo. I paid it a second visit on my fifth day, and went on to Livorno. Sixth day, at Livorno; went out to the lighthouse and saw the town, which does not contain much, but has more bustle and business than any other I have seen in Italy.

The seventh, I drove to Monte Nero, a few miles from

Leghorn, to see the country, and a chapel and the view. The eighth, stayed in passing three hours at Pisa, and slept at Pontedera ; and to-day, the ninth, arrived to dinner here. I have had fine cold frosty weather, good inns and fare, and have enjoyed it very much.

I dreamt the other night that my father, on seeing my little purchases, held them all rather cheap, but did not quite scold about them.

I bought a little, very little, Parmigiano of the British chaplain at Leghorn, which a Mr. Parker, of Lichfield and Bath, who has been in Italy for two years for his health, is sure as I am that my father will offer me at least five times the price I gave for it. *Nous verrons*, it travels in the packet of my blotting-paper book most conveniently. The day before I went to Pisa, I went with the Cowpers to see and hear an *improvisatrice*, the daughter of a physician here. She fired off on any subject that was given with wonderful quickness and cleverness, *bouts rimés* to suit several different subjects. She is, unfortunately, extremely ugly, and her voice not pleasant. I think her name was Langis or Mangei, or something like it. I should not wish to hear her again, especially as there was no escaping, and she did not tire for two good hours.

I was glad to hear about the Mound ; * it was certainly natural enough for them to wish to make the most of it they could for their pockets, but it is much better that they should not make much. I wrote to G. Vernon to get lodgings *for me* at home, and I have received an answer, telling me all about what he had done for himself, which is also perhaps natural enough, but not so satisfactory ; but luckily, before I burned his letter, I found at the end that he would secure some for me.

---

* A road across an estuary of the sea near Dunrobin. I imagine "them " to refer to the contractors or engineers engaged in making this mound.

I shall leave this on Tuesday, and get to Rome about the 14th. I wish we were to be all there together, to eat our Christmas pie.

LETTER XII.

December 8th.

I shall travel to Rome in company with the Campbells, so shall stop a day at Siena.

The death of the Duke of Mecklenburg seems to me to offer the queen the best opportunity of showing symptoms of relenting, and may make her think of her own mortality ; but I do not expect to hear of much good in that quarter. I have not yet written, and must do so now. So I take my leave of you for the present. My next letter will be from Rome.

Rome, December 16th, 1816.

Perhaps you may like to hear of our safe arrival here the evening before last.

I give the information as quickly as I can, as you may hear of M. Artaud, belonging to the French embassy, having been robbed, or at least attacked by robbers, near Monte Viterbo, a few days ago.

We heard of it on the road, but as it made it the more safe for us, in consequence of the guards being in search of the robbers, we were not so sorry to hear it.

He was attacked at ten at night, by four men. He fired, and they fired and ran off, and he continued his journey. I do not know if they have taken any of the robbers.

I wrote from Florence the day before I left it with the Campbells. We made as pleasant a journey as the bad roads and (at least, most part from Siena) an uninteresting country would allow ; we were *not* detained two days at a wretched inn at Radicofani, to wait till the torrents were passable, as General and Mrs. Ross were. I have only seen St. Peter's and the Vatican and Pantheon yet. Very good English society here. The town is worse as a town than I expected, but I expect to like it very much. I shall not go to Naples for a month at least, as I have my lodging for a month.

Lord Lansdowne has bought for £1100 a Venus of Canova, belonging to Lucien Bonaparte.

The post goes this morning, and I will not lose it, though you should learn nothing more than that I can date it from the Eternal City. I do not know what to see first. I think I shall go again to St. Peter's, and then to the Coliseum.

I shall write more at length in about ten days.

Letter XIII.

Rome, January 4th, 1817.

Since my arrival here, on the 14th of last month, of which I gave the earliest possible information, I have, of course, been occupied in seeing all day long all the things you saw here, and I suppose there is not much difference in the appearance of Rome since that time. The marble shops are full of pretty tazzas and vases and tables, which are very agreeable to visit, if the weather be too wet to go to ruins, etc., but generally it has been very fine and mild and pleasant.

I saw the Palazzo Doria two days ago, and was surprised by the *custode* accosting me on my entrance with this question about my name—" Lei è Stafford ? " I said, " E il nome del mio padre ;" on which he produced from his pocket-book a slip of paper with "Lord Stafford" on it, "E il mio padre." It turned out that he had been told by the English that Lord Stafford had a Raffaelle like one in the Doria collection, and he was delighted at finding a person who also belonged to this Lord Stafford; but how he came to hit upon me—whether he had asked the same question of every Englishman that came to see the pictures, or how, in short, it was, I know not, but it seemed odd.

I have had another adventure, which Roth calls very mysterious, which might have been more unpleasant—a writing-box stolen from my room, broken open, and left behind the street door, where it was found by the servant of the house, and brought to me the night before last.

The robbers selected whatever they found in gold, which luckily was not much—no money—a gold Venetian chain taken out of a pocket-book, a watch-chain, and some seals and rings attached to it; and a small box, which Lord William Bentinck had given me at Dunrobin to bring to a M. Artaud here, who had left Rome before my arrival, was opened and the contents taken. Pray communicate this misfortune to Lord William and my regrets. I had luckily taken out of the box, a few days before, the little pictures I mentioned, and some other things—letters, pocket-books, etc.—left. I have given an exact description of your seals to the police, but suppose I have not much chance of seeing them again.

I go on to Naples with the Campbells next Thursday, 9th. I received your second letter, of the 28th November, containing the bad accounts of the scarcity of food in Scotland; very distressing and melancholy.

The post seems the best mode of sending letters to you; indeed, there is no other from hence. I have not heard of anybody going home, except Mr. Brougham.

The Italian society seems very insignificant here. The

English live very agreeably together, and there are reunions at a foreign minister's or an English house almost every evening, but no balls or particular gaieties. Lady Westmoreland very hospitable.

I suppose this will find you in town. The Duchess of Devonshire is digging in the town, but not finding anything ; the Government are also digging, finding the old pavement and Gialloantico steps. Some of us, Lady Lansdowne chiefly, hunt over cabbage gardens and vineyards for marbles, and bring home bits of porphyry or giallo, and have little busts, etc., made of them. . . . Cardinal Castelpiante, who makes love to all the English ladies, cannot understand how there can be no scandal about them. He raves also of the charms of Madame Apponyi, the Austrian minister's wife, who is terribly affected, and not handsome. I should be sorry to live long at Rome as an inhabitant ; for a traveller it is very interesting and entertaining.

I see that the queen continues to enjoy the delights of Brighton as much as last year. I fear that nothing could have an effect on her, but a total prohibition of snuff. If this could fall into her hands, I would give more vent to my abhorrence of her hard-heartedness, but as it cannot, I will not dwell on such a disagreeable subject. I wish the times were better, and that my father would desire me to expend judiciously, in fine marbles and fine things for him, a good sum. I have seen Pauline Borghese,* with whom the Vernons are quite *coiffé*. She must have been very pretty—something like Lady Douglas, shorter, *passée*, and not *distinguée* in her manners. Direct to Rome. I shall perhaps write again before I go to Naples. Adieu.

* Pauline Bonaparte, Princess Borghese.

K

LETTER XIV.

Naples, January 13th, 1817.

I wrote from Rome about a week ago, saying that I should proceed hither with the Campbells. We set out a day sooner than we had fixed, on Wednesday instead of Thursday last, for the sake of Prince Henry of Prussia's escort. The Prussian consul at Rome, who had to order horses, etc., for him, and was to accompany him hither, having offered to order them for us at the same time, and the prince having allowed us to accompany him, we took advantage of so good an opportunity. The first night we stopped at Terracina, where the prince very kindly made us partake of his supper, as he did next night at Capua, whence we proceeded after supper; and as we had no lodgings provided for us here, we slept there, and next day came here.

My friend General Eustace, who had written about me to Lady Westmoreland, and to me, though I had not received his letter, has been so good as to lodge me with him. He has been here since March last, and has the pleasantest apartments possible in the Palazzo Cara-monica, close to the sea, and where rocks like a wall prevent fishers and washerwomen and lazzaroni from fre-quenting the shore, as they do in many other parts. The ' Campbells have got a lodging near the Ricci Teano Palace; very pleasant except for the great distance. The town is so full that it is extremely difficult to procure lodgings.

The opening of the new theatre of St. Carlo, which took place last night, and which has been looked forward to with much eagerness, was extremely splendid and brilliant. A magnificent theatre, lighted up with as many

candles as it could possibly hold—I believe nearer three
than two thousand candles. The Douglases invited us
to their box. It was the king's birthday. I went to court
in the morning, when, after nine hundred and sixty odd
subjects of his Majesty had kissed his hand, he desired
them to shut the door, and said that his hat was so tight
that it and the number of people passing made his head
ache. He had counted the number all the time.

We English were then presented. He was very civil,
and seemed very good-humoured, and after going round
the circle for a short time, said he must go to dine, wishing
us all good-bye and thanking us. His daughter, married
to the brother of the King of Sardinia, a frightful woman,
was with him.

Prince Leopold and his wife of Austria did not appear,
both being ill.

No Neapolitan ladies are allowed to go to the king's
court, but such as had been at the late queen's; consequently all such are old and frightful, and in much more
ill-shaped hoops and waists than with us. Just before I
left Rome I received your letter No. 4, mentioning
your others, one to Milan and two to Florence. I think
the Milan one must be a mistake, as the second Florence
letter mentioned that you had only written one before.

I have not heard from the Duke of Cumberland yet.
I think you had better not write to me, unless you should
have something pressing to write about immediately to
Rome, as I shall not be there, I think, long enough for
more than one letter to reach me there after you receive
this. I shall probably return from thence by Bologna, the
Mont Cenis, Lyons, and Paris. Perhaps a letter *poste
restante* at Bologna or Viterbo would be best for the present, and then at Lyons. At all events I shall inquire
at those places. Mount Vesuvius has a good deal of

snow, in spite of the fire which blazes fiercely at night.
Lady Douglas is not looking well, and, I believe, does not
think that the climate suits her.

After all, I do not at all wish to become an inhabitant
of Italy, but prefer the north of Europe.

14th.

Nothing to add to-day. The sea beats against the
wall, and sounds like at Dunrobin. Adieu.

LETTER XV.

Naples, February 10th, 1817.

On my arrival here I wrote to communicate the pleasing
intelligence. I received a few days ago your letter directed
to Rome of December 29th, for which I am very much
obliged. As I did not leave any money in England to pay
for subscriptions during my absence, I trust to having all
that advanced for me. I shall not be in want of any
additional abroad, as I shall not buy much, and I can
always draw on Drummond's for what I may want, as
they will make no difficulty of advancing my quarters
to me.

Henry Drummond is here for the sake of the climate—
very amusing with his inconsistencies about religion and
morality.

I have been very busy since I came, and am supposed
to have been more active in seeing all the sights than
anybody. I have been to Ischia for two nights, to
Paestum—much pleased with the temples—and to Bene-
ventum, where there is not much to see except a fine
triumphal arch of Trajan's, and I have seen most of the
surrounding country. General Eustace is an excellent

cicerone. I am staying for a grand masqued ball at court to-morrow, and a dinner at Circello's on Thursday, and shall take my departure from hence on Friday, the 14th.

I shall stay three weeks at Rome, and then, as I said before, through Bologna and Turin, Lyons, and Paris. I am sorry to hear that the postmaster at Rome has been detected and imprisoned for pocketing the payment of postage of letters, and burning the letters. As I think all mine have gone by the post, I fear they have shared the same fate with other people's. I wrote two from thence, I am sure, if not three. The Campbells went this morning. They had intended to have stayed for the ball, but she is not strong enough for any fatigue, so they determined to go, and make their way home by degrees. Her inability to take long walks has prevented them from seeing much. I think it would have been a better plan for them not to have travelled till next winter, instead of this.

I should have liked very much to have gone on to Sicily, but it would require too much time. Vesuvius has been very lively, and looks very grand at night. I had a fine day for ascending with Campbell and General Eustace, but we could not look down the crater, as the eruptions were too frequent and violent.

The weather has been most delightful ; always pleasant for an open carriage or a boat, except the day we returned from Ischia, which was rather wet and windy. Sir W. Cumming, I hear, preferred the views from the Calton Hill and Edinburgh to those from the most celebrated points here, and I prefer Dunrobin and the Sutherland coast to the Neapolitan, and the Golspie fishers to the lazzaroni.

11th.

Most of the persons who were at home are here or coming. The Vernons in a few days we shall probably meet on the road. This is rather an English day without sun, siroccoish. There are thirteen thousand Austrians in the kingdom to encourage loyalty. The Sicilians are much vexed at not being still under the English and Lord William Bentinck. The Neapolitan carnival is not particularly lively. Sir George Talbot's is nearly the only house where one has had opportunity of seeing the society of the place, as he has been giving balls constantly, and is supposed to be a *grand seigneur* of the first class. *Addio.*

I suppose the dining-room at Trentham is making a figure. The gallery at the Colonna Palace at Rome makes the best of any I have seen.

Lady John Campbell has turned Catholic, and is called a *principessa Scozzesa.*

LETTER XVI.

Rome, March 31st, 1817.

I am a little ashamed of writing again from hence, after having announced my intention of staying a very short time ; but as the Holy Week is so near, and one has heard so much of the ceremonies, and it may be for once only in one's life that the opportunity may offer of seeing them, and it will only make the difference of a few days, and as I shall not make any stay at Paris, I have determined to stay for them and to receive the pope's blessing, immediately after which I shall take my departure. I hope I shall give satisfaction in having the cypresses of proper proportion. It is lucky that Cippolino is preferred to porphyry, as porphyry cannot be had. Granite may ; but, as Cippolino is preferred, and can be had, they are to be of Cippolino accordingly. It has another advantage of being the cheapest, being the next easiest to work after marble.

I have been to see Palestrina, Ostia, Civita Vecchia, and to other places on the coast, which is too flat to be beautiful.

This month has been and is much colder than January and February were ; a good deal of fresh snow on the mountains, and sharp frosts every night.

I am annoyed with myself for having forbid you to send any more letters to me here. The Hopes are in great affliction at the loss of their second boy, after a long and distressing scarlet fever, of which there is no doubt but that he would have recovered if he had been properly treated. Unfortunately too many doctors were called in, and it ended with the death of the poor boy, after much suffering. Lady Westmoreland, who was of service in taking the others to her house, is inexhaustible on the subject. She leaves this for England in a few days.

I shall bring Elizabeth some music as a treat for her. I have not turned musician, though. I had a letter from Vernon two days ago on the same subject about which he has at the same time written to you, about Lord Elcho and Lady L——.

I saw the gentleman arriving here this morning, very dusty, and seeming to have travelled all night. I have no doubt they are very anxious to have all arranged smoothly, and I hope she will not have any more trouble or disappointment. She is *très douce* and amiable and pretty. G. Vernon has, I have no doubt, written to you at full length about it.

I have no travelling companions in view. The Campbells, I should hope, are arrived in England, and most persons return by Florence. I shall go by Ancona. Catalani is here, to sing, I suppose, after Easter.

There have been lately some vases and monuments found at Albano under a bed of tufa, and as there is no tradition of a volcanic eruption, they are supposed to be older than anything known of the sort. I have not seen them yet. Adieu.

In expectation of the pope's blessing, I send mine to the whole family.

I take care to finish my letter to-night, not to have to put to-morrow's date to it.

LETTER XVII.

Rome, December 3rd, 1818.

Having a few days ago given Charlotte an account of my being alive and well, and not having any news worth relating, I have not expedited any letter yet to you since my arrival here, and I have not received any from England since my departure, so I must content myself with hoping and trusting that papa, mamma, brothers, and sisters, etc., are all as well and prosperous as the detached branch of the family here. The delicious weather is a great *agrément.* Lord Morley's letters from England—and he seems to have the greatest number of letters of all the English here—give the same accounts from hence. I bought a Titian at Bologna, but it will not kill any of my father's (in the same way that my Correggio killed his copy by A. Carracci), so he need not be prematurely jealous. It is a little sketch of a portrait, about two inches square, and cost only four louis d'or.

December 4th, 1818.

Just heard of the death of the queen.* Sir H. Davy shot this morning a bird which he had never seen but in Orkney. Rome is very full of English of all sorts, and a great deal of sociability among them, and no quarrels that I have heard of. I have sat for my bust to Thorwaldsen, at G. Vernon's desire. He requires only four sittings of about an hour each, and does not measure with compasses, etc., as Nollekens did. The bust is reckoned like, and it is the last he intends ever to make, which sounds as if he had been much bored with it. Has my father got the "Villa Pliniana," a folio, two volumes in one, the engravings done above twenty years ago, but only published a year ago? I think not, in which case I had better buy it, as it is a fine book. Canova's "Nymph," for the prince regent, will probably have reached London before you go, or before this time. It is said to be beautiful. It is intended, at last, to search the Tiber.

Have you been to Teddesley yet? Pray, if you see or have any communication with Littleton,† tell him to write to me here. There are no accounts of robbers to entertain you with known here.

A merry Christmas and happy New Year.

LETTER XVIII.

Rome, Sunday night, April 4th, 1819.

My last letter was to Liz., and, I trust, safely received. I have not received any since, and have nothing very particular to write about; but I will not wait till I hear again lest you may think me idle.

* Queen Charlotte.
† Afterwards created Lord Hatherton.

We have heard of nothing for some time but of preparations for the visit of the emperor and empress, who
were received on Friday with great fuss. It is something
new to have the pope's palace filled with ladies and
courtiers. All the priests have been turned out for some
time to make room for the suite, and their rooms painted
with cupids and bows and arrows, and furnished with all
possible *recherche* and luxury. Everybody's cooks and
coachmen put in requisition. Pasquin has been active, too.
One morning it is said that over the entrance to the
Quirinal Palace was found, in large letters, "Albergo Pio."
There is a smaller Albergo Pio, kept by a Madame Pio, in
the Piazza di Spagna. Metternich occupies, of course, a
large share of the cardinals' civilities. Rome is in an exces-
sive bustle. The papal kitchens on *Friday* night, as I passed
by, were enough to make *one's mouth water*, as one could
look in at all the windows. I suppose that there was
seldom seen such a range of kitchens, with so many cooks
—I hope not spoiling the soups.

Lady Morley has been very ill of a twenty-one days'
fever since her return from Naples. I saw her to-day in a
state of convalescence, and doing as well as possible. He,
too, has had the gout.

We had some bad weather in March, which made
several people ill and abuse the climate of Rome, I think
very undeservedly ; for I believe that if one does not go
out of the hot sun into cold, damp churches, but take
proper exercise and not eat too much, it is as healthy a
place as any.

Lord Guildford, the Ponsonbys, and Lady B——, Dr.
Quin, Duke of Devonshire,* *cum multis aliis*, Lord and
Lady Belmore, who have been to Jerusalem and Nubia, are

---

* My mother's uncle—the " Magnificent " Duke—son of the famous
Duchess of Devonshire.

among the arrivals. Lady Westmoreland, I believe, set off this morning towards England.

I have read the two first volumes of "Marriage," and shall read the third when Lady Charlotte Bury lends it to me. Very good, I think. Pray, your little Ariosto from Dunrobin is not the Lyons edition of 1570, is it? because, if it is, it is scarce, and I have bought one here, a *little treasure.* We had a slight shock of earthquake, at four o'clock in the morning, about a fortnight ago. I did not feel it, I own; but at Trescani and Albano people left their beds and houses. The Duke of Devonshire means to remain till the middle of June. He is terribly deaf. The duchess has given me her book, which is pretty. Pray tell Mr. Grenville that I have a copy of Gower, which I intend for him, as he had been so good as to offer to accept it. When does Francis * take his degree?

Have you heard of a house, or part of a house, falling down behind the Hôtel de l'Europe here and crushing thirteen or fourteen travellers' carriages? The Ponsonbys lost two—quite smashed. Luckily no lives lost, and nobody hurt. An old woman had left her room for a certain purpose, which was to detain her only a moment, and in that moment the room went down.

Two travellers and a servant had gone that day to Tivoli, or would probably have been destroyed—what one calls providential!

LETTER XIX.

April 5th.

This morning's post brings me yours of the 15th, which I am delighted to receive. I must send this to the

* Lord Francis Gower, brother to the writer, afterwards created Earl of Ellesmere.

post.   The time passes so quickly here that I fear it may
appear some time since I wrote last ; but we have no interesting news to write about, and this is the least political
town in the world, though at present the Corps Diplomatique is strong, Prince Metternich and Kaunitz, Caraman
and Blacas, the foreign ministers at the imperial court,
having accompanied the empress, but it is said merely for
their amusement.   The mixture of Vienna society improves
the English.   Lady Sandwich receives every Saturday.
The emperor is said to be much bored with all the grandeur
and luxury of the preparations for him.   He stays three
weeks, I believe.   Maria Louise * only came to Temi.   It
was feared that the people would show her too much favour,
as happened at Venice.   Many thanks for averting the
execution at my palace.   I shall write again at the end of
the Holy Week.

At the commencement of the fourth part of these
letters, it will be seen that six years have elapsed, and
during that interval my father had married.   That most
happy event for both my parents took place at Devonshire
House on the 28th of May, 1823.   Of my dear mother I
have written in another place, and I will only here insert
some of her early letters, which, thanks to the kindness of
her nephew, George Howard (now Lord Carlisle, 1889),
were placed at Castle Howard at my disposal.   My only
regret is the small number that I found—there are but
four—but all are full of charm and the love of all things
of beauty in nature and art, that was always one of the
loveliest traits of her character and disposition.

In the first of these letters, written at the close of the
year 1820, my mother was in her fourteenth year ; the

----

* The second and unworthy wife of Napoleon.

"Grandpapa," with whom she describes walking up and down the gallery at Castle Howard, was Frederick, fifth Earl of Carlisle, so often mentioned in the Memoirs of last century. He had married, in 1770, Lady Caroline Gower, daughter of the first Marquis of Stafford, by which marriage my parents were nearly related. The old Earl died in 1824 ; he had seen and known all the celebrities of the latter half of the eighteenth century, and his recollections of Marie Antoinette and the French court must have been very vivid still when he discussed about those times with his granddaughter in the picture-gallery in their old Yorkshire home. He was succeeded by his son, George Howard, who was born in 1773. The sixth Earl of Carlisle married Lady Georgiana Cavendish, eldest daughter of the beautiful Duchess of Devonshire. It was he who, when Lord Morpeth, had been sent to negotiate with the Prussian court during the Napoleonic wars, and to whom my father had been attached, and whom he outstayed at the Prussian head-quarters in 1806-7.

Castle Howard, December, 14, 1820.

MAMA MIA,

Grandpapa is, I think, well, in good spirits, and particularly kind. I walked long and alone with him in the gallery ; he talked much of music—your music and Lady Granville's * that he admires so much. He regrets that so many married women should give it up as well as drawing. He means to establish celibacy in his family, among his granddaughters ; at least, such is his advice. He could not make me agree. He talked of the two Maries, so different ; of Elizabeth, possessing the qualities of a man, with all the vices of the weakest woman ; of Lady Jane

* Mother of the present (1890) Lord Granville, and sister of Lady Carlisle to whom the letter is addressed.

Grey, innocent victim of ambition; of Lady Salisbury, and La Comtesse Dubari, and her folly in not resigning one's self to a certain fate; of Marie Antoinette, effacing by a sublime death the faults of her youth; of "l'affaire du collier," Cardinal de Rohan, a complete fool; Madame Elizabeth, perfectly virtuous; of Madame Roland, a domineering woman; and many others who have illustrated the pages of their history, and whose good deeds shine more for being in a time when all but women seem to have forgotten whose children they were. As Shakespeare says—

> " How far that little candle throws his beams !
> So shines a good deed in a naughty world."

I began this before I received your letter, which delighted me. The room you sit in must be beautiful; I like Hardwick only by description very much. The pictures must be delightful, open books that amuse and instruct one. I cannot imagine anything like that lovely queen (Mary Stuart) but what is beautiful. . . .

I hope you will write to us often, and be as good a Boswellite as I am to you. Papa, Uncle Devonshire, Caro,* and George are more interesting to us than Doctor Johnson, David Hume, Joshua Reynolds, Garrick, and Goldsmith.

Yours,

HARRIET.

Extract of a Letter from HARRIET HOWARD *to her Mother.*

Castle Howard, August 7, 1821.

CARISSIMA MADRE,

The queen † still lives, but there seems little hope. It appears to me as if the death of celebrated people

---

* Her sister, Caroline Howard, afterwards Lady C. Lascelles
† Queen Caroline.

was reserved for the moment in which it will be an event of less importance, as the queen's would have been last year, and Napoleon's about ten years ago.

I like the way they have received Bertrand.* Those few and solitary instances of fidelity attached to misfortune deserve to be distinguished. . . .

Our garden in the wood has been covered with a stupendous urn. I rather regretted this. Shakespeare would describe it—

> ". . . a bank whereon the wild thyme blows,
> Where oxlips and the nodding violet grows,
> Quite over-canopied with lush woodbine,
> With sweet musk-roses and with eglantine."

Extract of a Letter from HARRIET HOWARD *to her Mother.*

Castle Howard, August 12, 1821.

What a delightful *séjour* Bowood must be! I think Lady Lansdowne such a stimulating person; I should like to live with a clever young man in the country, a little handsomer than Lord Lansdowne, though he really bordered on that at the Coronation with his hair quite fressy, and in his robes, which suited him particularly.

How interesting the account in the *Times* was yesterday! What courage the Queen showed!

Naworth, August 18, 1821.

Only think of me here! I can hardly believe it, though in an old tapestried drawing-room, close to the window that looks on the court of the old, venerable, interesting, and beautiful Naworth Castle.

But now listen to what preceded this journey. I left

* General Bertrand, after his return from attending Napoleon at St. Helena.

Castle Howard about half after ten, in the open barouche by Easingwald. A pretty road—I hear not the prettiest, but I admired the extensive view from Craig Castle, and was struck with the dreary, melancholy, and awful ridges of black Hamilton. In the first stage we were assailed by a heavy shower, the only one during our journey. We slept at Greta Bridge. The stage and the evening between Caterick and Greta were beautiful, the sun playing at bow-peep with the dark clouds that glided over the distant ridges of mountains. I was delighted with view from the *Inn* at Greta; it is although a pity should so perfectly resemble mutton broth. Rokeby seems a remarkably pretty place; and will always be an interesting one from *him* who has dwelt in it. I set actively and instantly to drawing an elm tree near the water; that now commands the entry into my sketch-book.

The next morning, accompanied by Charles,* that most civil of all civil persons, I sallied forth, and followed as far as possible down the banks of the river. What a beautiful and romantic country! I think it has great effect on one, and I do not know that, if my pencil had been a wand, Charles should not have been transformed, playing the Strephon and Chloe on these magnificent banks. How I like merry Carlisle, and the situation of Appleby Castle, and the view of Lowther on looking back after Penrith. Altogether, the road delighted me, and I enjoyed it excessively, the unobstructed view all around. What magnificent slopes of Wild Perfile, Saddleback, and Skydaw, the Cutter quite indistinct in the clouds! We drove in here by a new way through the park; the house comes more suddenly on one. I have already pounced on an oak tree for my fore-ground on that side; but I have not yet been out; for I began this as soon as I was up. I love this place already.

* Her brother, Charles Howard, father of the present Earl of Carlisle.

I cannot express the sensation I felt on entering the Hall, but exclaimed in George's words, "Ave, sacra Domus!" That stupendous fireplace awakens such a train of interesting ideas. Henry has just taken me up to Lord William's bedroom, library, and private chapel. In the first and last I inwardly blest the years that had elapsed since those days. In the second I admired the old venerable volumes, but deplored over the attention that chained him once over them and proved so fatal to the stranger's life, and, I should suppose, his lordship's future peace. But then the next instant I feel very differently, and wish we were still in those days "when beauty dealt the price which value won."

Castle Howard, October 21, 1821.

Absent or dead, still let my name be dear;
A sign the absent claim, the dead a tear.

Is not this a lovely practical fashion of beginning an epistle? It is just to show you the colour of my temper, for you not to think me "couleur de rose," when in reality I am "feuille-morte," and a sigh I will claim, though (you) are at magnificent Chatsworth with *your* lively and delightful uncle. I shall not call him mine till I have left the nest and launched in the skies and woods, for, as he justly remarks, we are not cursed in the land of the living.

Grandpapa, I am happy to tell you, is better, but he found last night the passage icy, and we again reassembled in the library. Grandpapa glancing over and abusing Mr. Dibden,* myself following Queen Elizabeth in her numerous ruinous and interesting progresses. The remaining trio at the card-table.

HARRIET ELIZABETH GEORGIANA HOWARD.

* Probably Dibden's account of his visit to Castle Howard.

L

PART IV.

From my Mother to LADY STAFFORD.

Hôtel de la Terrasse, Paris, April 10th, 1825.

DEAREST LADY STAFFORD,

I do not know what George has written to you, but I must run the risk of repetition to give myself the same pleasure. I long to hear from you and of the little one. Our journey was taken leisurely, but was a very pleasant one; the weather delightful, the inns we rested at comfortable, and the towns enchanted me. It seemed to me Prout need go no further than Beauvais for endless subjects of lake and yellow ochre houses. Paris surpasses even my expectations of its beauty, and that is saying a great deal, after having seen your drawings. We are perched very high, and not very comfortably. We think, if we can find better, of changing when our month here is over; a week had elapsed before we came. Lady Granville * is looking very well, much fatter, though slimmer in the waist, and in very high spirits. He is not, I think, in very good looks, though in very good health, and it is a great deal that the want of exercise does not affect that.

We dined with them the evening of our arrival; they

* Lord Granville was at this time the English ambassador at the court of France, and Lady Granville was my mother's aunt—daughter of the "beauti-ful" Duchess of Devonshire, and mother of the present Lord Granville, and of the authoress Lady Georgiana Fullerton.

were anxious we should meet some Scotch people. We were surprised at seeing Macpherson Grant walk into the room, and Glengarry's lusty form, attired in a tight suit of tartan, with a sword, and thistles up to his ears. Lady Caroline Wortley and Lady W. Bentinck dropped in after dinner, also several French ladies, but we went away too early to see the greatest *élégantes*. The house is delightful, but the furniture much tarnished.

I was much pleased the next day with my drive down the Boulevards to the Jardin des Plantes. The weather is beautiful, and uncommonly hot. We sat very warm at Lady Granville's without a fire. We went to the Italian Opera last night. We made several visits together to-day, but only found Madame de Jarnac at home. I was a little surprised with the voice, the shadow of the frame, and the smartness of the dress. I need not tell you that I had many inquiries to answer, and that she sends you many loves. We dine with her Thursday. We walked afterwards in the groves of the Tuileries, which have rapidly covered themselves with light green since we have seen them; the walks were covered with the prettiest-dressed crowd I have ever seen.

We were at chapel this morning at the *ambassade*. Leopold * came, looking very old. He is much *épris* with a young, pretty, and infantine Countess Potoska. The Duchess of Somerset is here, but we have not, fortunately, seen her yet. I was much pleased at being made to know Soult.

LETTER II.

Paris, April 12th, 1825.

I went to court yesterday, and my reception there was most cordial. The king shook my hand, which is, as my

---

* Prince Leopold of Coburg, afterwards King of the Belgians.

father will say, very unusual. He inquired after you both, and was as friendly as possible. It was the anniversary of his first return to Paris in 1814.* The nuncio made an address on the part of the Corps Diplomatique on the occasion, to which he answered. The first two sentences of the reply were remarkably well delivered ; then, unluckily, the king was obliged to look at a paper in his hat again, and then he could not read it exactly, and was out of his lesson. He did not seem to mind it much, but laughed, and went on with great energy of will and expression ; and if he had but been more perfect in the recollection of it, his delivery would have been admirable. He looks a little older, but very hearty.

The dauphin was also very civil, and desired me to give you his compliments ; and so was Madame. The Duchesse de Berri was, as she always is, very insignificant-looking. She never says anything to people presented to her, particularly to English, whom she is supposed not to like. In the evening we went with Lady Granville to Madame de Gontaut's—not a *soirée*, but one or two people sitting with her; and then to Madame Juste de Noailles', whose evening it was, of the same sort as those we used to go to. Lady Granville says that Harriet is very much admired ; but we do not mean to be vain of it, as we do not admire much in return. The *sacre* is fixed for the 29th of May.

The two or three last days have brought out some green leaves on the trees, but rain is much wanted, and seems likely soon to come. We are smothered with dust ; the immense quantity of new buildings everywhere, and of pulling down the old, adds much to this dust.

* Louis XVIII., who died this year (see p. 98).

LETTER III.

From my Mother to LADY STAFFORD.

Campagne Watteville, Geneva,
Sunday, August 13th, 1826.

DEAREST LADY STAFFORD,

We are now quite happy and comfortable in our new habitation, and the children are well again. We moved last Wednesday. The house, though old, is clean and very airy; the view from all the windows delightful, particularly from our pleasant bedroom upstairs. The dining-room opens to the garden, which is shady, and allows the little women to be out almost all day. The little terrace is delightful, bordered with pomegranates; at one end is a temple-seat, where we sit out late, and have given and drank tea. On Thursday we dined some way off with Mr. Gallifé, who gave us a very hospitable dinner, and a dessert on some dishes given him by Elizabeth. On Friday we had the Baths alone at dinner, their belongings being gone to Chamouny. On Saturday morning we went to see Ferney. Two rooms are preserved in the same state, hung with bad pictures and common prints.*

---

* On their way to Switzerland, my parents visited the field of the battle of Waterloo. I find the following account of that visit in my mother's diary : "The road from Brussels is beautifully wooded. While rattling over the 'Chausseé,' it was painful to think of the many wounded who must have been agonized on that road. We stopped at the village to see the church, where many of the brave dead are buried. Among them Frederick Howard [my mother's uncle],[1] with an inscription to the effect that it was put up by his regiment, the 10th Hussars, but that his mutilated remains had been carried to England at the desire of his father. The spot where my uncle fell was marked by three trees, now no longer standing. One of them, under which,

---

[1] Byron's "young and gallant Howard."

LETTER IV.

Carlsbad, Monday morning, July 28th, 1828.

We arrived here the day before yesterday. The journey from Frankfort is altogether tiresome, though there are some parts of fine forest landscape, a large palace at Aschaffenburg, of the beginning of the seventeenth century, with some good pictures in it, and a fine garden, with a terrace over the Main. The queen-dowager had left Würzburg the week before. The palace there is very large and handsome ; a magnificent staircase, with a ceiling painted by Tiepolo. We slept at Aschaffenburg ; Würzburg ; Bamberg, where is shown the window in the palace from whence Berthier fell (it is a fearful height) ; Bayreuth, near which we saw the Hermitage, a country house, or two houses, built fancifully by Frederick's sister and her husband, and now in the original state, and with several portraits and pretty gardens ; at Eyra, a very dirty inn in a dirty town, with the views of an interesting old castle with a Roman square tower ; and thence over a

according to our guide, the Duke of Wellington had stood, had been bought by an Englishman." At Liege she writes of a grand mass in the cathedral : "The first I ever heard. The mummery of the quickly gabbled-over Latin prayers, the bowing to one another, the turning, the kissing, the bending, are too ridiculous for even pomp of place or ancient date of worship to blind me for a moment. The pomp of place, however, I do not object to, as I see no harm in devoting to God the most beautiful and successful efforts of man's labour. The danger is that it may lead to substituting mere outward things for the religion of the heart ; and this is undoubtedly the system, nay, the very end, of the Catholic religion." My mother's delight with the scenery of the Rhine was extreme. From Cologne they went up the Rhine ; to Darmstadt, Heidelberg ("there is a delightful mixture of beauty in this splendid ruin "), on to Baden, Bâsle, Neufchâtel, and to Geneva ; passing the summer months at the Campagne Watteville, close by its beautiful lake. That autumn they visited Italy. At Bologna they made the acquaintance of the celebrated linguist Mezzofanti, not then yet a cardinal. "The Abbate is fluent in his English," she writes, "which is perfectly correct, spoken slowly, and with some degree of foreign accent."

very bad road, two long stages, hither, where we are glad
to be in clean, large, airy apartments.   There is a fine hill
and wood close about the place, chiefly spruce firs ; and it
is entertaining, for a little while, to see the crowds of
drinkers at the different springs.   They begin at four
o'clock, and continue in succession to drink till seven or
eight, walking all the time to assist the waters, of which
they drink from ten to fifteen glasses in the morning.   We
dined yesterday with the Prince Auguste in the *restau-
rateur's salon,* which was full of people of all nations—one
Pole in the old costume of the country, now almost
discontinued.   It is rich, but not handsome, I think.
There are not many English, I believe, and none that we
know.

I told Prince Auguste how much obliged you were for
the print.   Dinner is going on in the *salon* from twelve
to three, at different tables, for large or small societies.
People seem to breakfast very much out of doors, and after
dinner they sit out all about the place, drinking coffee and
smoking.

There are very pretty walks through the woods, and
those that drink the waters are to walk as much as they
can, so that there is a constant movement.   We are called
at six every morning.   The music and other noise in the
street would prevent one's repose continuing uninterrupted
till a later hour.   Harriet * is entertained with it all.   We
have found Pahlen † and the elder Prince Schwarzenberg,
the heir of the title, here, who are very useful in showing
the place, etc.   Pahlen goes to-morrow to Dresden.

* My mother.
† Count Pahlen, a lifelong friend of my father's.

LETTER V.

Toeplitz, Thursday, August 7th, 1828.

We arrived here the day before yesterday. We left Carlsbad on Monday, and slept at a place a little out of the road, called Schönhoven, where a Count Tihernin has a very pretty, large garden. This place was very full lately ; but the King of Prussia left it last week, and its visitors have since dispersed.

We are to dine to-day with Prince Clary, the proprietor of the country hereabouts. His mother is the eldest daughter of the old Prince de Ligne, and I knew her and her son a little at Vienna. We shall stay till Saturday, when, if it be fine, we shall embark at Aussig, and go down the Elbe two stages to a place called Schandau, to see the Saxon Switzerland. We shall then stay a few days at Dresden.

I found at Carlsbad some old acquaintances. The weather was hardly fine enough to make the place en-joyable, as it ought to be in summer. The hills are covered with spruce firs, some oak and beech, bilberries and strawberries, with delightful walks. The mornings were very cold and the weather changeable. There are fine views of hills and from hills all hereabouts.

I was very glad to receive yesterday your letter of the 24th. The last English newspaper I saw at Carlsbad was of the 17th, with the debate in the House of Lords on Lord Holland's motion. It is very difficult to see any newspapers here. I am sorry for the hay in England, and fear that other crops may suffer too, as the weather does not appear to be settled yet. Prince Auguste expressed his hope that the Grevilles would visit him at Brussels again this year. He was very civil to us.

LETTER VI.

August 8th, 1828, Evelyn's birthday, etc.

We dined at three o'clock yesterday. The old princess, *née* De Ligne, is ill and confined to her bed, which I am sorry for, as her I know best of the Clary family. They are, however, very civil, and proposed to drive after dinner, for which purpose the *reganté* called for us at five. Her daughters and some young men followed in two or three other carriages, and we drove to a very prettily situated ruin, from whence the view over all the valley, and of hills and of ruins and villages, is very fine. She invited us to pass the *soirée* and drink tea at nine o'clock. I went ; Harriet rested at home. They are to call for us again this evening to show the environs, and to-morrow we shall proceed.

LETTER VII.

Dresden, August 16, 1828.

I wrote last week from Toeplitz, after I had received your letter from London. We have since then seen some beautiful country in descending the Elbe from Aussig. We slept one night at Teschin, and were delighted with Count Thun's *château*, which, you may remember, Francis was much pleased with. It is a building of great extent, having forty-two windows in a line on the side which looks down the river, and, I suppose, as many on the other, and a great number on each of the other sides (the forty-two take a side and a half, I believe, in this sort of way, and the river winds about it). Harriet, very properly, shakes her head, and discourages my attempt to sketch it. *Pourvu que* she can do anything better, it is very well.

The next day we passed and slept two nights at Schandau, from whence we took two drives and walks to see beautiful views.

The next day we came down the Elbe to Pirna. We left the boats about an hour's walk above the town, because the wind became contrary and made the water rough. We met the carriages at Pirna and came on to Dresden.

We are, of course, delighted with the pictures, and have been to the gallery every morning. We always dine at two o'clock, drive out after dinner, shop, go to the Opera —at least, have been there this evening. It was Italian ; began at six, and ended at half-past eight. Some of the royal family were there ; and the dowager-queen had discernment and curiosity enough to send to our side of the house to inquire who we were, as Pahlen was informed by some one of his acquaintance. We had the curiosity yesterday to see the palace, which, I believe, few people think of doing, as there is in fact nothing to see in it (I mean in the inhabited part of it, as everybody goes to see one part called the green vaults, where all the valuables of the Crown and all the absurd magnificence in trinkets and finery of Augustus III. is placed) ; but the palace is an extraordinary building, very large, having many separate dwellings attached to it by passages over streets, without any respectability of architecture, and consisting of many large rooms not much connected—the rooms occupied by the late king, very dirty and uncomfortable, and the queen having to pass through her *salon* to go from her bedroom to her dressing-room ; the Princess Augusta, the only child of the late king and queen, living in two small rooms looking into a narrow street, and having to pass through the great dining-room to go from the queen's apartment to her own. No pictures in the palace, though so many and good are placed so high in the crowded gallery that they cannot be well seen. All the doors of the apartments occupied by the royal family have the initial letters of the three kings written in chalk by the priests, with the date of the year when they were thus sanctified. The king never allowed the queen, they said, or anybody else to come into one of his rooms, which we saw ; the next to it his library, which was filled with music-books.

Lord and Lady Warwick, with Lady C. Ashley and Dr. Jones, have passed through, going to Vienna and Italy. We mean to leave the children here, and to go to Prague, and into Silesia by Glatz, and return hither through Lusatia (?), or shall stay at a place called Schmeideberg, to see some of my old acquaintances, Princess Louis Radzivil and Princess Guillaume of Prussia, who both live in that neighbourhood. We shall be here again within three weeks. Harriet has had no headaches and is very well ; so are the children. Elizabeth rather thinner, and Evelyn fatter.

Sunday, 17th.

We are going to see the Catholic Church, and the royal family return from it through a corridor over the street to the palace, so I must seal this and send it to the post.

Ever affectionately.

Any letter written very soon may be directed hither, but any in September to *Poste restante*, Berlin. We shall be there about the middle of September.

P.S.—I have just received your letter of the 4th instant, with a good account from Trentham, and Harriet has a good one from Westhill,* both of which give us great pleasure.

* This was a villa near Putney—the site of which Napoleon I. is said to have determined to build his Imperial Palace on after the conquest of England !—which my parents lived in for some years. It is now a home for incurables.

LETTER VIII.

LADY GOWER *to* LADY STAFFORD.

Glatz, August 23rd, 1828.

DEAREST LADY STAFFORD,

We left Prague early yesterday morning, after having passed there two very pleasant days. It is the most interesting and outlandish town I have seen during this journey, and has a *soupçon* of a barbarous look which does not displease one *en passant*. Some of its views are magnificent, chiefly that looking over the town from the height on which the palace is situated, and from the bridge. The bridge itself is delightful, and we enjoyed it to perfection on a fine moonlight evening, which showed to greatest advantage the colossal statues of saints that border it on either side, among them their patron, St. John Népomucène, distinguishable from the rest by the many lighted tapers, and by the respect the busy population never fail to pay. The Moldau is a fine and rushing river. The old castellated walls that run along the steep have a picturesque appearance; the *tout-ensemble*, with its spires and trees, towers, gateways, and palaces, is very fine. Daylight shows one that there is a touch of decay over the whole, but this allows one to exaggerate the idea of what it may once have been. It is natural that it should be so, as their noblesse desert it for Vienna.

The Schwarzenbergs have a fine palace; the Lichtensteins had, but have sold it. The royal palace is immense, and has some fine Bassanos. Driving about has a take off in the extreme steepness of the hills within and without the town. We found the Prince Auguste D'Arenberg, who was as usual all good nature and civility, notwithstanding a fall from his horse he had had a day or two before, and which must have caused him great suffering.   Half his face was patched up.   He had heard reports of the Russian army having had *des pertes effroyables*, and of the emperor being returned to Odessa after having been half-way to Constantinople.   I hope it is not so.   We slept again at Toeplitz, between Dresden and Prague.   Few things can be finer than the view over Bohemia from the heights of Zalm (?).   I have often wished for your power of drawing what is delighting one.   We left the children at Dresden, and expected to be back within three weeks.   I liked it from its pictures and collections, and seeing the armoury is living ten minutes in another age.   The pictures do not give one the enchantment of those at Bologna ; they are ill seen.   The town disappoints one ; there is nothing to examine, or interest, or admire in modern German architecture.   I have often felt glad to think Lord Stafford has rejected for York House * a style whose ornaments and decorations so nearly approach this German taste.

We saw a great deal of Pahlen, who is good-natured and entertaining, but he appears not happy.   Had he been born in another country, or had he now the means of living where he liked, this might not be.   We slept at Shonigingnatz (?) yesterday, and have had a hilly journey to-day to this place.   The country is fertile, and hills well wooded.   I shall be anxious to hear of Francis's new life ; it must be arduous, but having real useful ends and the prospect of good to be gradually done must be stimulating to activity and exertion.   Is there a chance of our hearing of Lilleshall from you ?   We hope so.

Good-bye, my dear Lady Stafford.   Pray remember me very kindly to Lord Dover, and believe me,

Ever affectionately yours,
HARRIET GOWER.

* Now Stafford House.

LETTER IX.

Schmeideberg, August 26, 1828.

I must begin a letter to-day (though I shall not send it for a day or two, as Harriet wrote to you from Glatz two days ago) because I have this morning received yours of the 12th, for which I must thank you. It is very agreeable to hear so good an account from Trentham of everything excepting weather, which is very bad with us here too. We had two very fine days for seeing Prague, but yesterday was very bad for seeing this country, where the mountains are reckoned beautiful, but they have been so covered with clouds and fog that we cannot judge of them. Trentham must certainly improve every day in its beauty, and the new additions make it a very fine place, as well as very pretty. Prince Radzivil, who has just been here, says that they have had but one fine day since the 10th of August, when they came here. We are going to dine with them at three o'clock. She, you know, is the Princess Louise,* of whom you have heard me and others talk. They are in great affliction, having lost a second son last year, who was just going to marry in a very desirable way, and in the winter the wife of the eldest son died, and after that a child she had left, which was with them ; besides a great disappointment in the failure of the marriage of their eldest daughter with the King of Prussia's second son,† which had been long intended, but has been broken off, it is thought at the instigation of the Empress-mother of Russia, who did not like a Radzivil to have precedence before her granddaughter, and the circumstance of the Princess Royal of Prussia not having any children made some awkwardness about the prospect of a

* Of Prussia.   † The late Emperor William of Germany.

M

queen not of full sovereign blood, so that it has been
settled that the king's son is to marry a princess of
Weimar ; and all this has had a bad effect on the health
of the young Princess Radzivil, and is a sad affair.

LETTER X.

Friday, August 29th, 1828.

Rain, constant rain without ceasing, ever since we
arrived here, which prevents one from going out much in
the morning. We dine alternately at the Radzivils' and
Prince William's. The first have a pretty enough villa
within a mile ; the latter a good château house within
three miles' distance, which he has bought, and at which
they live most of the year, staying till the 18th of December, when they are obliged to go to Berlin. They have
furnished it very comfortably, in a solid, handsome, simple
manner. They are all much pleased with Harriet. Dinner
takes place about four o'clock, then tea, then supper at
nine o'clock, so that one can eat as much as one likes ; and
we come home about ten.

We shall stay till Tuesday, and on that day return
towards Dresden, whence we have good accounts to-day,
as well as in a letter from Westhill, of all the children.
There are to be grand manœuvres here in the beginning
of September, but if this weather last it will be wretched
pastime for spectators as well as actors, and if it were fine
it might be too long a fatigue for Harriet, and therefore I
think it better not to think of them. It seems very extraordinary to be again in so much of Memel society, as
these two princesses were always with the queen there,
and both very much attached to her. Of course we talk
much over old times. It is now just twenty years since I

left Memel, and fourteen since I saw Princess Louise at Berlin. She is, notwithstanding her distresses, which I mentioned above, and some anxiety about the health of her eldest daughter, on whose nerves the return to this place (where the brother died when they were here last) has had an effect for the time—she is still a most agreeable, lively, and clever person, *ætat* fifty-eight. Princess William was at Memel, a year younger than Harriet is now, and always amiable and excellent. Prince Radzivil is a Pole, with much talent for drawing portraits; and for music Prince William, very gentlemanlike, quiet, amiable, and served very gallantly in the campaigns. (You will think my letter becomes like one of Princess Elizabeth's.)

We heard, at Prague, bad accounts of the Russian army. The Austrian wish was father to the thought, at least, here such accounts dare not come. But the Turks are very strong at Schumla. The season advances, and there is yet much to be done before they are driven out of Europe. The answer to this will find us at Berlin, where we intend to be on the 15th, and shall probably be till the end of September.

LETTER XI.

Berlin, September 19th, 1828.

- I wrote from Leipsic, whence we next day reached Wittenberg, and on Saturday last Potsdam, where we remained Sunday and saw the palaces, etc. On Monday, the 15th, we came here, and found very good lodgings in an agreeable situation, and fruit and flowers as an attention to Harriet from Count Redern, who has also brought up his mother from the country to give a dinner and civilities. We dined on Monday with Sir Brook Taylor, and on

Tuesday with the Cumberlands.* She is looking, I think, very well ; fatter than may be good for health, and complains of never feeling free from a liability to vertigo. The duke was, as usual, very friendly ; Prince George not quite well, with something aguish. She took Harriet upstairs to see him. Sir B. Taylor and the rest of the mission (poor devils, as the duke calls them when addressing them), and Lords Bloomfield and Clanwilliam,† who met us at Potsdam, dined there. Next morning the duke called on Harriet, and we met him at dinner at Count Redern's.

There is now assembled here a meeting of the *savants* of Germany, to the number of nearly four hundred. Humboldt directs the proceedings regarding them, and opened their *séance* yesterday morning with a speech. In the evening there was a sort of *fête* in the great concert-room for them, at which we assisted. The *savants* and military were assembled in the room below ; the king and some of the royal family in part of a gallery which makes a royal box ; we in the other parts of the gallery. It was a musical affair. The prince royal came to me and made acquaintance with Harriet. He seems very lively and very good-natured, but terribly fat for so young a man. The king has hardly been in Berlin yet, and his chamberlain, who is with the Princess Leignitz, is not yet arrived, so that we have not yet had any communication with him, and I fear we shall have to trundle down to Potsdam for that honour, which it would have been more agreeable to have had here. But he is going there to-day for the manœuvres, which will last all next week.

---

* Ernest Augustus, fifth son of George III., who, on the death of his brother, William IV., became King of Hanover. His wife described here was a Princess of Mecklenburg-Strelitz, who married the Duke of Cumberland as her third husband.

† Ambassador at Berlin, 1823-28.

20th.

This town has been improved since I was here, and several new buildings raised ; and, indeed, what I consider the best part of Berlin is what we have left in Silesia.

LETTER XII.

London, September 9th, 1831.

Madame, comment se trouve t'elle ? after the ball of last night.

We are not the worse for the coronation, though it was a long affair.

The princesses and ladies, who sat opposite to the peers, looked very well and splendid ; but it lasted too long, and there was no order or attention to the getting away, so that one had to wait long in a crowd, coroneted and wigged and others, all pushed about by the soldiers of the guard, who had to come out too. In other respects it all did very well, except that there was not space for all the waiting on and supporting and attending the king and queen, so that the great officers, etc., seemed as if they were crowding round to smother them. Harriet's dress was thought very good, and Loch and Morpeth and other admirers praised her appearance. There were several peeresses who are not usual ornaments in court circles— Ladies Ferrers, Poltimore. *Harrington* was expected, but I believe was not there. The rest were "stars indeed, though some are falling," as was the case in former times.

Harriet sat next to Lady *Stafford*, Lord Byron divided me from Lord Stafford, and old Lady Talbot of Malahide, said to be past eighty, was next to Lady Dover. Dowager

Countess Paulet and Lady Keith * were oddish-looking.
Dowager Richmond † at the head in gold, the young
Duchess of Richmond in silver, looked very ladylike ;
the Duchess of St. Alban's ‡ very magnificent. Montrose
sat at a respectful distance from her, and looked as if she
feared a breach of quarantine on her part (nobody spoke a
word to St. Alban's). We dined at home afterwards. Had
the Carlisles—he a good deal tired—and Cavendishes and
Morpeth.

There were fireworks in Hyde Park from nine till
eleven, to the great delight of the children.

LETTER XIII.

Brighton,§ January 6th, 1833.

Before dinner his Majesty called me, and asked whether
I had heard from my father or mother since I came here.
I said that I had heard of his Majesty's great kindness
to my father. He said that was what he meant ; asked
what title it was to be—whether Stafford. At dinner, after
the first glass of wine, he said, "The Princess Augusta ‖ has
suggested to me what I think a very good suggestion—
that your father's title should be Sutherland." I bowed

* Lady Keith, in her own right, was perhaps better known as Madame de
Flahault, wife of Count de Flahault de la Billardrie, who was for some time
French ambassador at the court of St. James's.

† The Duchess of Richmond who gave the ball at Burnett's on the eve of
Waterloo.

‡ Formerly Miss Mellon, the actress, widow of Mr. Coutts, the banker.

§ King William IV. and Queen Adelaide were keeping Court at Brighton
during the winter succeeding the passing of the Reform Bill. The first election
on the new franchise was just over, and Lord Grey had been returned to power
with an increased majority. Lord Stafford (the father of the writer) and Lord
Cleveland were advanced in the peerage to dukedoms in recognition of their
support of the Liberal ministry.

Sister of William IV.

and acquiesced in the opinion of its being a good suggestion, and that I was sure my father would be very happy to hear what his Majesty might suggest. He said, "Pray tell him that I think so, and send an express to him for the purpose." Then he asked me again to drink, and said, "I drink to the healths of the Duke and Duchess of Sutherland." The next glass that he drank with me, he said, was the first we had drank together since I had become the son of a duke.

He afterwards told me that he had brought me out into the world. I agreed that he had always shown me the greatest kindness. He talked of Wemyss being ill, and asked me, if I had no other engagement, to come and dine again to-morrow, and he would ask Wemyss to meet me. He was very cordial—interested about the moving into Bridgewater House, which I had to tell him of in consequence of his asking where I lived in town.

The queen does not work on Sundays, but draws, and the Duke of Devonshire had to sit facing her for an hour and a half to have his portrait drawn by her Majesty in her book. I was rather alarmed at having the book opened at the queen's desire to show me a portrait. Luckily I knew it immediately to be the Duchess of Cambridge (some of them were not guessed so easily). I shall send this by coach, that you may be acquainted with his Majesty's suggestion. It is no secret now. Lord Albemarle, before dinner, said to me that he yielded precedence to me with very great pleasure, that Lord Grey had told him of the dukedom, and that he was very happy at it.

It would have been *droll* if we had been able to have announced "the elevation" to you. It cannot be any longer much of a secret, as the king has told Sir M. Tierney of it, who has told Lord de Ros, who has told—and so on. I wrote our names at the Pavilion yesterday, and am to-day invited to dine. We have taken a house, as the hotel is very cold and not comfortable. The house is like all the others in the same row, Brunswick Terrace (No. 26), but it is better furnished, and has even a steam apparatus like that at Westhill.

I dined yesterday at the Duke of Devonshire's with the Dovers. Harriet had a headache, and did not. She is very well to-day. We heard of Madame de Vaudemond's illness from Dover, as Pozzo * had told Lady Holland that she was not expected to outlive the night. She is, indeed, a very great loss.

Lord Grey told the Duke of Devonshire of the duke-doms (you know that Lord Cleveland is also to be one) after dinner on Friday, with great glee, as a secret. The duke began soon after hinting about it to Lady Dover, when Lord Grey came up and told her only to tell Lord Dover. She told him that the Gowers had just come, and supposed she might tell them. The Duke of Devonshire hoped that the title would be Sutherland. We also think it the best. The weather is very cold, and my hand is unsteady after walking. Dover seemed much better.

LETTER XIV.

Brighton, January 8th, 1833.

I am sorry to have been out of the way, in case of any probability of being of any use in *the present crisis.* My being here has, however, given the opportunity for the king's kindness being shown on the occasion, which may give as much satisfaction as my being with you could have done, as I shall not have an opportunity of communicating

* Pozzo di Borgo.

again with his Majesty personally till to-morrow (when I am again invited to meet Pozzo). I shall write a note to Princess Augusta, and inclose your letter to her. The Duke of Devonshire took the queen in to dinner yesterday. I sat on her left, and we *got on*, I think, extremely well on several subjects—pictures, fine arts, Germany, begging letters, and charity, and she means to request your assistance for a bazaar for the society to assist foreigners in distress.

After dinner there was a tiresome game of commerce, at which the king and Princess Augusta, Lord Albemarle, Lady Mary Fox, and Lady A. Kennedy, and Lady Kilmaine, Miss Cavendish, Colonel Wemyss, the Duke of Devonshire, and I played for nearly an hour and a half. Lady Dover also dined, and after dinner worked at the queen's table with three or four ladies. The dinners are always large, as there are twenty-seven inmates or family besides us strangers.

I have no sort of wish to change my denomination, and think not changing may be most convenient. I must be wholly guided by whatever my father may think and say about it. The king said, "He becomes Marquis of Stafford," to Princess Augusta, but of course he cannot care about it, so it must remain entirely with my father. *A propos* of the title, it will, I think, give satisfaction to our friends in Scotland, and can give umbrage to none, and it is fortunate that all agree in preferring it. In talking it over here, and the possibility of any awkwardness in the possible event of hereafter there being a Duke and an Earl of Sutherland in different branches, it occurred that another patent, giving also the title of Duke of Staffordshire, or whatever it might be, would be a resource, and that having it a *separate patent* would make it unnecessary to use it except in such a case as that, for which it might, as it were, be reserved.   I do not know if this observation be worth communicating, but there can be no harm in my doing so. I am very glad that Mr. Grenville was in the way to be consulted.

LETTER XV.

Brighton, January 10th, 1833.

I enclose a proof of what his Majesty's wish is regarding my denomination, and before dinner yesterday he called out, "Lord Stafford !"   So I stepped forward, and he said, "You intend, of course, to be called Stafford ? "   I said, bowing, that there had been no determination yet come to about what I should be, and he said, "I think you ought to be so, and *I have called* you by that title ; " so I said that of course his Majesty's wish decided it, and I suppose it is better to be let be accordingly.

The double title in the same patent would not have answered the purpose.   A separate patent would have been, I believe, the way to have obviated the possible difficulty. Perhaps that may be yet done when there may be occasion, if so be that it should occur.

The Duke of Devon told me that he had mentioned to the king the possibility of the dukedom and earldom being in two persons, and that the king did not think it should be a difficulty or objection to the title.

It was a large party yesterday.   The king was not much disposed to receive Pozzo very cordially, but he seemed to be civil to him ; told him to sit by Princess Augusta, and questioned him after dinner about his life, and had him at his whist with Princess Augusta and Lady Anne Maria Doutin.   Pozzo is gone to-day.   He asked me and several others to dine again to-day.

Trentham is amused at the idea of his being *pa*, and said, laughing at it, "Lord Gower is sitting on Lord Stafford's knee." Another idea was that my umbrella, etc., belong to him ; that he supposes Frederick * will become Trentham as soon as *he has teeth.*

Lord Western dined at the Pavilion yesterday. It would have been right, they say, to have come down to wait on his Majesty if my father's health had allowed it, so that my being here serves, perhaps, as a sort of demonstration of respect. We have fine cold weather ; the sea very pleasant to look on. Palmerston stays to-day.

LETTER XVI.

Brighton, January 11th, 1833.

Nothing very remarkable occurred yesterday at the Pavilion. The king desired me to sit on one side of the queen, who was taken in to dinner by Ludolf. One could not be at a place better fitted for the purpose of familiarizing one to a new name, as the king seems to enjoy calling one by it, and the others follow the example very gravely. The king and Princess Augusta and I and seven others played at commerce ; another commerce table for the more noisy part of his family and suite.

The queen always works, and Lady Dover takes work *in her glove* very ingeniously for the evening, which lasts till near twelve.

Harriet entertained Lord Dover here.

---

* My brother Frederick, who died off Scutari at the commencement of the Crimean War (see "My Reminiscences ").

LETTER XVII.

Brighton, January 15th, 1833.

I met Talleyrand * and Madame de Dino † yesterday at dinner at the Pavilion, and he stays to-day, breaking an appointment with Palmerston and with Lord Grey, with which he acquainted the king, and told him that he therefore could not stay to-day unless " votre Majesté l'ordonne ; " and the king said, " Eh bien, je l'ordonne," and I saw them together this morning at the Albion Hotel.

There is a very great dinner at the Pavilion to-day, for the Duke of Gloucester, with all the officers of the Blues. Lady Dover ‡ and I go together to the party at night.

The king yesterday told me he had signed the *warrant* for my father (which sounded odd).   I expressed my father's regrets at his health not allowing him to come to express in person, etc., etc.

LETTER XVIII.

From my Mother to the Duchess Countess.§

Brighton.

DEAREST DUCHESS,

I have some difficulty in impressing upon myself who it is that I am addressing so familiarly, yet this is

* Talleyrand was at this period French ambassador at the court of St. James's. He was appointed after the Revolution of July, and was now approaching his eightieth year. Palmerston was Foreign Secretary in Lord Grey's cabinet.

† The Duchesse de Dino was Talleyrand's niece, and was granted the rank of Ambassadress in accordance with the precedent which had occurred when Talleyrand was accredited to the Austrian court.

‡ Lady Georgiana Howard, sister-in-law of the writer, and the wife of the first Lord Dover, who died at an early age a few months later.

§ My grandmother having been Countess of Sutherland in her own right, was, after the elevation of her husband to a dukedom, known as the Duchess-Countess of Sutherland.

not so strange to me as feeling at home with your late name. I have some illusions, such as thinking that I draw beautifully ; that I have a right to authority over George, and a considerable share in M. de Talleyrand's affections— I, who feel as if I was much richer ; but this does not signify, as I feel wiser at the same time, and therefore did not buy immediately, as I might have done but for this latter quality, the most beautiful *bijou* of an Italian villa we went to see yesterday. Saying it is the prettiest thing in Brighton is too poor praise for it. It is the only very pretty, plain bit of the simple Italian architecture I had ever seen in England, with its three windows *rapproché* in the middle, the one on each side at a distance, with little terraces, balustrades, parterres, and a dolphin fountain, all built and arranged by Barry, the architect of the Travellers' Club.

My Monday was a brilliant post-day to me, as I got your letter and one from mamma, with an account of the dinner. She was much pleased at its success, and amused me with the greatest show of titles in the smallest space. For example : " Let me, whilst it is fresh, give you a sketch of the evening at Stafford House, my dear lady marchioness ; but I cannot yet quite accustom myself, and when they ask for Lady Stafford I point to the duchess."

END OF PART IV.

PART V.

Harriet Howard, Countess Gower,
afterwards Duchess of Sutherland,
and her eldest daughter, Elizabeth afterwards Duchess of Argyll

N

These two letters are from my mother to the Duchess Countess, her mother-in-law, on hearing of the dangerous illness of her husband, the recently created Duke of Sutherland ; the next after hearing of his death at Dunrobin. "Elizabeth" is Lady Westminster; "Francis," Lord Francis Gower, subsequently Lord Ellesmere ; and "Charlotte," Lady Surrey, afterwards Duchess of Norfolk.

LETTER I.

Bridgewater House, Monday, July 22nd, 1833.

MY DEAR DUCHESS,

⟋ I cannot say how deeply I feel your kindness in writing to me in such very anxious moments. I do believe in the power of your mind to be calm in danger, and not to allow hope a hold that would unfit you for a return. I need not tell you what I feel for you in these trying times of existence, nor for the duke, whom I love so affectionately, and from whom I have received a kindness that has always touched me with gratitude. I trust, if God wills the worst, that George and Charlotte will have the satisfaction of being with you *both*, and that, if it pleases God he should recover, I shall feel for their happiness in being with you at such a time of thanksgiving. Still I am aware it must be a state of most anxious doubt. I thanked God to find that the state of pain had abated.

Yours ever affectionately,
H. STAFFORD.

N

LETTER II.

Bridgewater House, Wednesday, July 24th, 1833.

MY DEAREST DUCHESS,

However prepared, the shock and emotion that your dear and most valued letter caused has been very great. I long to hear that your health has not suffered from the exertions that are made while life lasts, and by the misery that death must cause. My dearest duchess, it is comforting to think that he died in your arms, and that the struggling spirit is at peace. I have copied your letter for Elizabeth, for I could not part with it; and I have written to Francis. God bless you, dearest. I regret very deeply that George and Charlotte could not be with you at such a time.

Believe me, yours ever affectionately,

H. STAFFORD.

s

From my Father to my Mother.

LETTER III.

Dunrobin, July 30th, 1833.

DEAREST LOVE,

We have just returned from Dornoch. It has been a very striking and extraordinary scene. Between eighty and one hundred of the principal tenants and gentry were assembled in the lower room here by half-past ten. Loch came for me, and Surrey and E. Howard went with me into the room, when Mr. Kennedy prayed on the occasion. Then wine and cake were handed round, while the coffin was brought into the court; and then I, as chief mourner, at the head, and Edward Howard, as next nearest descendant, at the foot, and Surrey and William Howard, Loch and Mackenzie, and Young and Gunn (the head of the clan Gunn, by the way, claims the privilege of bearing the pall for the Earls of Sutherland), as pall-bearers, conducted it to the hearse, which then proceeded to Dornoch, followed by my father's carriages with the household, by four or five mourning coaches containing the clergy, by about forty carriages and gigs of gentry and tenants, and about one hundred on horseback.*

The road from the avenue to the further extremity of Rhives Plantation was lined on the right hand by a row of men of the common people, all from Kildonan and Loth, their heads uncovered, and with their hats before their faces, while the *cortége* passed, as if they were each of them praying.

At Kirkton the same line began again, of the people of Rogart and Assynt, and from Tongue and the Reay Country, which continued all along to [illegible] Farm, across the mound, while groups of women and children were on the heights and rocks at different places. About a mile on this side of Dornoch the same thing again, and nearer Dornoch they lined the road on both sides; all

---

* Dying at Dunrobin, my grandfather was buried in the cathedral of Dornoch, the old burial-place of his wife's ancestry. He had probably intended that his bones should rest at Trentham, and had there erected one of those gloomy-looking buildings for the dead known as a mausoleum, which most of the great English country places are made hideous with. These buildings have neither the sanctity of propinquity with a church, nor the simplicity that should make the last resting-place of our mortality appeal to the survivors. It was a far happier feeling that inspired my mother's uncle, the Duke of Devonshire, to choose the place for his interment in the midst of his tenantry in the quiet little churchyard at Edensor, under a simple stone. To know that one will be expected to be entombed in a niche of a huge building is enough to add another terror to death; and the day, I hope, is not far distant when rich and poor alike will agree in thinking that cremation is the best and most sensible form of returning to dust and ashes.

uncovered and serious, and appearing impressed with the solemnity of the ceremony, so that the whole time appeared one of devotion, in which above three thousand partook. One felt sorry not to be able to give something to each as one passed, and that one would have wished to have been a pope to have given them a blessing. Where the road winds up the hill, on the other side of the mound, on looking back, one saw these good people returning quietly home in bodies over the moor. There was no whisky given. The aisle of the cathedral appears built for the purpose of the monument, which is at present like a great altar, raised on two steps, of very imposing proportion. The coffin is put into it at the head, and there is space within it for three or four. Mr. Ramsay performed the English funeral service, and after we stayed to see the tomb closed with large flagstones and hard brick and stucco ; and then the church emptied, and we came back by Embo and Skelbo, to avoid the crowd. The conduct of the common people is really wonderful ; not a sound to be heard all the way. The sun shone bright and hot. I thought much of Trentham * at the tomb, and how I should have felt *had it been he*, and felt that one must do all the good one can, and then the rest is of little moment. We come to our wealth, etc., certainly at a time that disposes us to such thought ; and it is better for ourselves that we do so than if we had been younger, and perhaps too much occupied with the thoughts of enjoying all this ; though there is no reason, I think, why we should not enjoy it all very much too. In short, dearest love, I hope and trust that you will have much enjoyment, and of the purest sort.

My mother wishes me to visit the Reay's Country and

---

* The present duke, whose title was Trentham till my grandfather was created Duke of Sutherland.

Strathnaver; if I do, it will take a week to do it, so shall see.

Ever, dearest love, most affectionately thine.

LETTER IV.

Bridgewater House, August 2nd, 1833.

MY DEAR DUCHESS,

I cannot say how touched I am with your kindness in writing to me as you do, and in knowing that George has been a consolation to you. If he sees that you are better, it will do him good; for his humility never acknowledges the blessings he confers by his goodness and his amiability, and this I know from my own experience. But that nothing can turn the first current of your great affliction, I well know, and that a great blank in existence must be felt by the great loss of one to whom you devoted care, thought, and affection. Charlotte must and deserves to be a comfort. I never saw a person more unselfish, and entirely devoted to you both. Georgiana * talks of you very often, with great interest and affection. To see the broken existence of this poor young being, whom I love most fondly, must affect mine. But I do not believe we are the worse for these sad wakings from the dream of life, and the having to break to her *his* immediate danger.

To her sanguine-hearted and gentle spirit that was a moment of such pain as few others could imagine or realize.

Blanche † is going on perfectly well, and their happiness

* In this letter from my mother to the Duchess Countess, she mentions Georgiana, who was my mother's sister, who had married Lord Dover, a man of much culture and literary ability; he died in early life, in 1833.

† Blanche, another of my mother's sisters, was Lady Burlington, whose

is, I think, fixed on a solid basis. Mamma is still rather suffering, and goes to Brighton to-morrow. Francis has been most amiable and distressed at the melancholy details I gave him. He sets out to-morrow for Dunrobin.

Believe me, my dear duchess,

Ever affectionately, gratefully yours,

H. G.

LETTER V.

Tuesday.

MY DEAREST MOTHER,*

I am much distressed at not having been with you, and not being with you now ; but Charlotte and I will both be with you as soon as possible.

I feel what a severe trial this is for you, and much vexed not to be with you at this time, and fear you expected me sooner ; but I do not think that I could have come off sooner under the circumstances as known to us at that distance, but I must lament my absence extremely.

Charlotte will be a great comfort and blessing to you. She is very well. I know how much you will suffer at this affliction, and also know your spirit, and the resources of your mind, and your courage, and I have *lately seen* instances of resignation and courage which encourage me to confide in YOURS, and everything has been done that possibly could be, and my father's former illness had been such as to make one grateful that he should have been enabled to enjoy his life, as he certainly has done since, and I really think that he may be counted among the most

early death in 1840 was a calamity to her family, who adored her. She was the mother of Lord Hartington, whose recent birth is here referred to.

  * This letter, which has no date, must have been written by my father to his mother on his way to Dunrobin, where he arrived after his father's death.

fortunate of men in so many respects ; but we shall be with you, I hope, nearly as soon as this.

> Ever most affectionately.

LETTER VI.

Bridgewater House, August 5th, 1833.

MY DEAREST DUCHESS,

It was a relief to me to receive to-day the accounts of one of the most agitating days you have had to go through.

George wrote, too, a beautiful and very affecting account of that day. It was well it was there, my dear duchess, in the vast privacy of his own lands, among a good, simple, religious, and grateful people. I was glad to hear that it is your intention to employ Chantrey,* who is sure to succeed after that fine bust.

My dear duchess, I deeply feel and value your kindness.

> Yours ever affectionately,
>
> H. G.

LETTER VII.

Bridgewater House, August 20th, 1833.

MY DEAR DUCHESS,

I have a most kind letter to thank you for, and it gives me great satisfaction to hear that you are able to be much out, and that you think of going out among your people. I have great belief in the good effects of exertion, and particularly when it is directed for the good of others ; and you will feel how much you are following the duke's

---

* This refers to the monument which was afterwards placed on a hill in Trentham Park, and is a well-known landmark in Staffordshire.

steps, and fulfilling his wishes. You will begin by exerting yourself, and after a while, I hope, enjoyment may again return to you.

I trust that you will not have thought for one moment of George's being away from me. I know him to be usefully employed, and that he is happy to be with you, and I think he will return to me with an additional stock of health.

I pray God to preserve him this first of blessings, without which all the good things of this life would be as nothing to me.

Then, my dear duchess, I am engaged, and usefully. I mentioned to Georgiana your idea of a uniform edition of his works. She seemed pleased, and said she had thought of it. You will have received from George the papers which I got immediately, and as many, I hope, as you desired.

LETTER VIII.

Trentham, October 26th, 1833.

Your letter of the 24th is extremely kind and considerate, and, as you say, we are all so well off that there can be no cause for uneasiness in any respect with regard to any of our worldly goods, of which there is such a plentiful abundance for us. I must tell you that [illegible] at Dunrobin mentioned your wish to give up the diamonds. Harriet had determined to advise you not to do so, thinking that they had better remain in your hands ; and of course, as soon as any shadow of a doubt of the propriety of your giving them crossed your mind, there could be no question about it ; and I only wish to assure you that we do not grudge them to you in the least possible degree, and only hope that you will not think about them except as yours. And as to the *plate*, I wish you to consult your own taste, as of course you will do, as much in the use of it as in the ordering it, as Harriet, whom you think of in considering the subject very kindly, cannot have any anxieties on that subject. I say all this that you may remove from your mind any feeling that may in the least interfere with having a full enjoyment of your own.

Yours affectionately.

LETTER IX.

Trentham, December 14th, 1833.

We had the satisfaction of finding the children well yesterday. We saw the garden chamber on Thursday ; did not like the shapes of the vases, but think that a terrace and balustrade garden must be a great improvement to the place.

We were very comfortable at Hardwick, which is entirely unlike anything else. With thick curtains and large fires, the house was really comfortable. The gallery, into which we looked next morning, is very grand and imposing, and well covered with portraits. The large, old-furnished bedrooms, hall, etc., are very striking and interesting, and you would be delighted with it. We went to see Keddlestone,* in the hall of which the columns are very fine ; but I do not like the material, the Derbyshire alabaster, and think they look too much like painted wood. There are some good rooms in the house, but in the taste of Adams, and it did not look enjoyable. We ordered four iron gates at a foundry at Derby, and arrived here between seven and eight.

* Keddlestone is Lord Scarsdale's place in Derbyshire.

LETTER X.

Trentham, January 20th, 1834.

We went to-day to Alton Towers, not knowing that the Shrewsburys had returned, and found them at home.

We were very much struck with the magnificent entry, through a long, high, well-furnished armoury, picture-gallery full of pictures, a chapter-house sort of hall, then a conservatory full of plants and statues, and then a drawing-room and gallery, looking very comfortable and habitable. All these and the other rooms were warm and agreeable, and, though they were alone there, all appeared used and lived in every day ; and when the entrance-door opens, a harper is playing at the entrance, a porter equipped as such opens the doors, and three or four livery and out of livery servants are all at their posts. He is adding a drawing-room and libraries and state bedroom, and another picture-gallery. The chapel, eighty feet long, and high in proportion, with stained glass, and all cased with oak, is very imposing and solemn.

They gave us a very good luncheon, and we then walked in the garden, which is very beautiful and astonishing, and well kept, with marble statues, all out unprotected all this winter ; and though it was a grey day, and no sunshine, but some drizzling rain, it looked very cheerful—so green, well mowed, walks in good order. There are some buildings which might be spared, but altogether it is full of entertainment, and very agreeable to see ; and they are very good-natured, and we are pleased to have found them, as it was a duty, and we saw it all much better and more agreeably than if they had not been there.

LETTER XI.

Star and Garter, Richmond, August 3rd, 1834.

DEAREST DUCHESS,

As you desired, I took the bracelet to Madame de Lieven * the day before yesterday (Friday). She was to embark in the evening. We had met them at Lord Palmerston's the day before, and I settled with Lady Cowper † to call for her the next day. She was dreadfully overcome at receiving it, *des sanglots*, and expressed beautifully all she felt of gratitude to you from whom the idea originated. I am sure it gratified her very much, and I am quite glad you thought of it. To see her depart so broken-hearted was really affecting. Madame de Dino was also of the last dinner-party. She talked of you, and looked very handsome. Not so the chancellor, who also talked of you with admiration and of his project of visiting you. The upper rooms at Stafford House are delightful, and I am much pleased with an idea inspired by George of a whispering pipe between my room and Elizabeth's. We drove over to Westhill yesterday to see the children, and found them very comfortable. Trentham used your fire-engine with such immoderate delight that he made his nose bleed. He is to be a little restricted. He is a picture of perfect joyousness when occupied with it. Good-bye, my dearest duchess. I long to hear of you at your journey's end.

Lady Montague desired me to express her regrets to

* The wife of the Russian ambassador, whose withdrawal from the court of St. James's was in consequence of Lord Palmerston's nomination, as British ambassador to St. Petersburg, Stratford Canning, contrary to the wishes of the Tsar.

† Lady Cowper, the sister of Lord Melbourne, became Lady Palmerston in 1839, after the death of her first husband.

you that she did not see you before she went.   George has made many persons happy with your drawings, among others the chancellor, who halloed out to me his thanks from an open carriage, with Miss Spalding and Mrs. Petre.

Ever affectionately yours.

Extracts from Letters of my Father to his Mother.

LETTER XII.

London, June 25th, 1835.

Did you hear what Cobbett * said, not long before his death, when some one remarked that Lord Brougham had been put on the shelf?   He said, " Put him on the shelf! You might as well talk of putting a live rat on the shelf! "

June 27th, 1835.

We had a little trial of French horns and of singing by Lablache and Tamburini yesterday on the staircase, and it was thought very fine.   Miss Berry was reminded of the " last trumpet " by it ; and then we sat down, above forty, to a breakfast which was many people's dinner.   Lady Morley thought it might do for a marriage breakfast for Mr. Grenville and Miss Berry.

LETTER XIII.

Stafford House, July 6th, 1835.

The affair here last night was perfectly satisfactory in every respect (except Mr. Grenville's being prevented by a cold from coming).

* William Cobbett, the well-known Radical writer, only attained his ambition of entering Parliament at the general election of 1832, shortly before this date.

The music was excellent, and said to do better than at the Opera, and the company behaved well. The Duchess of Cambridge made a good object for attention, without engrossing too much, and most people said it was the finest thing of the sort they had seen. It lasted late, and we did not get to bed till nearer four than three.

I had a sit-down table in my room for the Duchess of Cambridge (the others eat on their legs). The cold suppers were very good, dessert looking well and luxuriant; the rooms well lighted, as well as the hall, and no crowd or confusion. Trentham went about very independently, at one time sitting by Lord Hill * in the side gallery, and not going to bed till the end of the first act.

Harriet looked very well, and was thought to do the honours in a distinguished manner. I wish you could have been here. We had sofas reserved for Carlisles, Lady Pembroke, and Clanwilliam. The children (Mrs. Granville Vernon as an infirm invalid) in the western gallery, near Harriet's rooms.

Harriet took Lord Grey to supper between the acts, and the Duke of Wellington after the concert, and we showed her rooms afterwards to the Duchess of Cambridge and the Duke of Wellington.

In the middle of the first act the Dowager Lady Salisbury was promenaded up the stairs on Grunow's arm. The foreigners were all struck with the scene generally.

We had put looking-glasses opposite to the openings to the staircase in the corridors, which have a very good effect, both by day and night.

The gas-lighting from the outside of the lantern did beautifully for the upper part of the staircase.

* The Peninsular and Waterloo hero, at this period Commander-in-Chief.

LETTER XIV.

Paris, October 5th, 1835.

The dinner at the Tuileries was very large. People think it not so good or well served as our king's.

They receive after dinner during all the evening.

The king has (at Sebastiani's desire and, I believe, at that of the Duke of Nemours, to whom Harriet had expressed her wish) invited us to see Versailles with him— *un insigne honneur*, as I believe it has hardly been shown to any stranger (the Duke of Orleans took Lord Clanri-carde there, and Lord Munster has been), and is not to be opened till March. He is doing a vast deal there, making it a sort of museum for old French historical remains, and it is, I believe, very well worth seeing.

They are also very civil in sending the order for the box at the Opera and play.

LETTER XV.

Paris, October 29th, 1835.

Madame de Lieven had a very intimate talk with Talleyrand, and says she hopes to take the place of all the old friends he has lost. She wishes very much to have her friends with her ; and it is likely to be a very good place to see different people of the best society, as the Broglies are very attentive to her, and M. de Barante, and Thiers, and ministers here and foreign, etc., are all often with her.

On Tuesday we dined at our *ambassade*, to go after dinner to the Tuileries, to join the king and queen and the King and Queen of the Belgians, much as they used to be round a working-table. The king very civil, and the King of Belgians, too, inquiring much after you.

One goes through the Galerie de Diane to go to the apartments in which they receive, which are handsome. We have to-day received an invitation to dine at court on Saturday, at six, and one from the Broglies for Thursday, the 5th of November. We went there after the Tuileries.

Madame de Broglie has become rather like Madame de Staël, in a turban ; Madame de Lieven says she has been most amiable to her, and she likes her very much.

LETTER XVI.

Paris, Saturday, November 7th, 1835.

While the impression of what we have seen to-day is still fresh, I must write to tell you that Versailles is more than ever it was a wonder of the world. And we have seen it in an unusual way, having had the honours of it done to us as completely (by the *padrone*) as possible.

Sebastiani came to us at half-past ten, and went there with us. We were shown up the Escalier des Princes into an apartment which used to be that of the late Duke and Duchess of Orleans, with a comfortable fire, glasses of water and sugar, and a retiring-room adjoining.

In about twenty minutes the court arrived (le Roi des Belges and Duc de Nemours * had gone to shoot at St. Germains) ; the queen, Madame Adelaide, the Queen of

* King Leopold of the Belgians, the uncle of the Queen and the Prince Consort, whose first wife was Princess Charlotte of Wales, married as his second wife, in 1832, Princess Louise of Orleans, eldest daughter of King Louis-Philippe. The Duc de Nemours, in 1840, brought about another alliance between the Saxe-Coburg Gotha and Orleans families by marrying King Leopold's niece, the Princess Victoria. The Duc de Nemours had himself refused the throne of Belgium in 1831.

the Belgians, and her sisters, and the Prince de Joinville, and
gentlemen-officers, and their ladies accompanied the king.

The king desired Mr. Nepoen, the architect, who had
already shown us the general plan of the alterations, to
explain them as we went through ; and all proceeded
over the *château*, beginning with the Aile du Midi, in
which you remember visiting Madame de Polignac, which
I told the king, who called some one to ask where her
rooms exactly were.

The whole of that wing is quite altered. For instance,
in one part thirty-six different rooms have been thrown
together into two rooms on different floors. In other parts
of the palace were high windows, apparently one on the
outside—were in fact divided, so as to give light to three
(if not four) stories. The intermediate floors have been
removed and long galleries constructed, viz. in the lower
range ; statues from old monuments and busts of celebrated
French people are placed without end ; rooms one after
another are fitted to receive immense pictures, many of
which were done for Bonaparte, of his battles and the
whole history of France under monarchy, republic, and
empire ; and monarchy, again, is represented as fully as
possible.

A series of all the *connétables*, of all the *maréchaux*, etc.,
etc. Louis XIV.'s bedroom is restored to its original
condition, so that he would find himself as much at home
in it as if nothing had happened. The original bed (recovered from Naples), balustrade, coverlid (given by
Madame de Maintenon, and worked very badly by her
ladies at St. Cyr, and which had, since the Restoration,
been conveyed to Antwerp, and has been recovered by
Louis-Philippe), is on it ; and everything, or imitation of
everything, just as in his time.

We had luncheon in Louis XV.'s room, in which he

died. The Aile du Nord is all being internally recon-structed, to receive pictures in its immense range of rooms. There is an endless collection of old portraits not yet arranged, which, after our walking for above four hours through the palace, it became too dark for us to see in detail. Indeed, the whole was hurried, and only seen in a transient manner.

All the rooms in the centre body are filled with Louis XIV.'s battles, by Van der Meulen and others. All the ceilings restored, or newly painted and gilt.

Marie Antoinette's rooms have been put into the state in which she inhabited them.

Marble columns have been found inclosed in walls below, where alterations on former occasions had taken place ; and the palace is now intended to become a great historical, national museum, to gratify the national pride, and make it the national wish to preserve it as a grand monument, as the temper of the times and habits of the people would no more have made it a suitable residence. It seems a very good idea of the king to preserve the edifice by rendering it such a national object of interest ; and it certainly never was as magnificent as at present, and we must have walked some miles in it.

There were little carriages of two chairs opposite to each other, or little platforms with wheels, which the servants drew through the rooms for the ladies ; but the king was so kind in showing everything, and talking of everything to us, that Harriet did not take advantage of them. She had, unfor-tunately, a very bad cold, which prevented the full enjoy-ment she would have had. But we have returned as from another world, full of admiration, and feeling very much obliged by the kindness shown to us.

Harriet at the Broglie dinner had Maréchal Maison by her, who talked of *his* picture at Versailles, and of what the

O

king was doing there, and said, "Vous pourrez le voir dans deux ans," " Pas avant ce temps, et non pas plus tôt." She did not tell him then that he was mistaken, but it entertained Sebastiani to hear this.   We are very much obliged for his kindness, though he says he had no merit, for that the king (with whom Sebastiani is in much favour) immediately said to her that he had shown it to nobody, and did not intend it till it was finished, but that "pour la Duchess de Sutherland c'étoit une autre chose," and that he should be happy to show it (so that is as near being shown it by Louis XIV. as can be in these times, you see, and there certainly is a likeness, though *you* will say no comparison, but I own I prefer the present).

People send family pictures and statues to add to the collection. Those that do not like one part of the historical recollections are proud of another.   It is altogether a flattering history of the country, especially as all defeats and failures are unnoticed.

One ought to have read St. Simon just before going to Louis XIV.'s rooms.

We had no time for the gardens.   The alterations are all internal.

The king appears in very good spirits and health, and much interested in this work, which is, I believe, his chief *délassement.*

LETTER XVII.

Paris, November 20th, 1835.

We dined at Talleyrand's on Wednesday. A numerous party ; the table being of the shape of the dining-room, nearly square, and only leaving room for the service round it.

It is odd that the stone floor is uncovered.   Little

pieces of carpet are put before some of the ladies' chairs, but not enough for all, at the great dinners, and people are seen to change colour from cold feet during the repast. I took in Madame de Valencay.

LETTER XVIII.

Paris, November 22nd, 1835.

Harriet had a long visit from the Duke of Nemours yesterday. He is a very well-behaved, rather old-fashioned and provincial sort of mannered young prince—shy, but very civil, and, we suppose, rather an admirer of madame la duchess ; but as I was also at home yesterday, it did not appear sufficiently decided for me to be sure of it.

Madame de Lieven says that Harriet always dresses remarkably well, but this may be in return for some Trentham grapes which I sent her.

LETTER XIX.

Paris, November 26th, 1835.

Yesterday we dined at Mr. Rothschild's ; and that you may not think we lose caste, or do what *you* would not like us to do, I will tell you that the party consisted of the Duc de Broglie, Talleyrand, and Madame de Dino, the Granvilles, the Austrian and Russian ambassadors, Lord Carlisle, and Prince and Princess Schönberg (*née* Schwarzenburg, a very lively, agreeable little person, with a very *retroussé* nose, in manner and conversation and size reminding us very much of Elizabeth), and Madame Rothschild's mother and sister ; so I hope you will see that we were good company.

The dinner was good, but lasted long for a French

dinner, and the *luxe* is great and amusing ; the apartment all furnished in the *goût de la renaissance* in imitation of Henri Deux's time, with a mixture of Louis XIII. and XIV.

There was a concert afterwards.

I tell you of all our dinners, as G. Harcourt used to mention his.

We saw a fine diamond to-day, larger than any we are personally acquainted with, but we think that we have enough.

The villain Lacenaire, who is in prison and to be executed soon, and who is said to have committed fifteen murders, *and after* the last gave a dinner at a restaurant, has written some beautiful verses since his condemnation (which, however, I have not seen, but Talleyrand had a copy of them), full of love for all mankind, and as if he had the best and tenderest of hearts !

He used to write vaudevilles.

LETTER XX.

Paris, December 3rd, 1835.

I saw Lord W. Bentinck yesterday, soon after his arrival. He said he had two very pleasant dinners *chez vous*, and that nobody, either here or in London, was half so agreeable as you ; but he denies absolutely having even declared himself against primogeniture, as he says that in truth he has not made up his mind on the subject, and cannot consider it to be best, but being a younger son, and not having a family, he has not the prejudices in favour of it which are natural to those other ways circumstanced ; that when it was in question here he bought and read twenty different pamphlets on the subject, but could not bring his mind to a decision positively.

We went to the opening of the Chamber on Monday. We were obliged to go at eleven to secure places, and the king did not come till half-past one ; but Harriet went with Elizabeth's likeness and little Princess Schönberg, whom she likes very much, so that she did not find it very long. The king delivered his speech (which we think a good one) distinctly. He was well received in the Chamber, but without demonstrations, I believe, on his way ; and the children were not satisfied with his *cortége*, it being much inferior to our display on similar occasions. They had a good view from our windows as he passed by the house. We went in the course of the evening to Mons. de Broglie, it being his first reception. The room was full, chiefly of deputies ; she looked pretty, and was very civil and friendly to Harriet. I dine with the Duc de Broglie on Tuesday or Saturday evening, and go to the reception at the Tuileries. There were five people arrested on Tuesday, before the king's going to the Chamber ; it was said two were to be disguised as women, and to give a petition to the king and shoot him at the time of his passing. A disagreeable sort of position, that he cannot show himself without risk ; and still more so for the queen, who must be in constant anxiety for him. They seem to bungle about bringing the people to trial for high treason.

LETTER XXI.

LADY E. GOWER * *to her Grandmother, the* DUCHESS
COUNTESS OF SUTHERLAND.

No date ; probably December, 1835.   Hôtel Lobau.

DEAREST GRANDMAMMA,

I like Paris very much indeed, but I shall be
very glad to go to England to see you again. We have been
to see almost everything at Paris. There is a very beautiful
new diorama.

I have been several times to the play. I was very much
delighted every time, but still more than any at "Norma,"
where Mdlle. Grisi acted.

It is excessively cold here. I have had very bad chil-
blains, which have prevented me walking for some days,
but they are much better now. I like the Louvre better,
better than anything else at Paris. We have been there
seven or eight times.

I like the "Belle Jardinière," by Raphael, better than all
the other pictures.

We went to four cathedrals on our way to Paris—
Canterbury, Abbeville, Beauvais, and St. Denis. Mr. Wood
showed us Canterbury Cathedral, and explained everything
to us.

I have a drawing-master here. I like his lessons very
much indeed, and M. Taglioni teaches us to dance.

Good-bye, dearest grandmamma.

Believe me ever your most affectionate

ELIZABETH L. GOWER.

* Elizabeth Gower (afterwards Duchess of Argyll), born in 1824.

LETTER XXII.

Paris, December 4th, 1835.

In the first place I must tell you that the grouse and black game arrived quite safe and fresh, notwithstanding the weather having been mild lately, and they have been very much liked. They must have been very well packed.

What a shocking catastrophe at Hatfield !* I am very glad that you have been enjoying your visit to C—— so much. I almost wonder you do not go for two days to Farnham, unless you are afraid of the hospitality being bad for digestion.

We dined on Monday at the Apponys, who are very civil, good people, and it was agreeable—not numerous. Yesterday I went to the Chambre des Pairs, and heard M. Cremieux defend the prisoners from Luneville, and the *procureur* sum up against them ; so it was a good day for my purpose, of hearing something of it, and for seeing the new Chambre, which has been built for the occasion, but is, I believe, likely to be more lasting.

It is a handsome *salle*, but said not to be good for hearing.

The Granvilles and Mr. Ellice are to accompany the king to Versailles on Saturday. I should think Mr. Ellice likely to suit the king, as he can give him so much information about all he has lately seen.

Do you ever see anything of Lord and Lady Holland ? It is a pity, I think, that that house, which is sometimes the most agreeable I know, should be no resource to you, for whom they both have so much regard—and they would enjoy dining at yours so much.

* The burning of the west wing of Hatfield House, when the Dowager Lady Salisbury perished in the flames.

Lord Carlisle and family have moved into a very pretty small house, looking on the Champs Elysées (by the way, do you make the plural *s* of Champs Elysé with the *e* of Elysées? Because Talleyrand and Madame de Lieven do not ; and they do not say *pa sencore*, but *pa encore.* Which do you ?), belonging to a Duchesse de Sans, next door to one Miss Berry had.

Lady Carlisle stays at the ambassade.

Have you not at times had dealings with De la Lauti, a picture-dealer ? Rothschild gives him a high character. I wonder if Lord Farnborough thinks well of him ?

LETTER XXIII.

Paris, December 13th, 1835.

I am very glad that you have got a copy " to your mind " of Sir R. Gordon for the Duke of Bedford. He has always been kind in sending to us his books, " Woburn Marbles," etc., so that it is quite right to be attentive to him.

I am sorry to hear of your child ; take care in this desperate weather. We have had uncommon cold ; now thawing, with a thick fog. (I have just been called to see Trentham go to his bed. He sends you his " love and a kiss." He would like to go to Dunrobin, not every year only, but every month, he says.)

Mr. Ellice has had accounts from the Greys, which makes it possible they may come here. Madame de Lieven and M. de Flahault are much excited at the idea of his coming. He has not been for near fifty years, but all feel a difficulty about encouraging him to come, as the [illegible] will be received with great distinction by the king, and many people here think he may be " put out " about some things, *imprimis* a lodging, which it is so very difficult to get in Paris at present that the Mouchys do not come on account of the difficulty, and Lady Charles Grenville, after much looking about, has settled with Lady W. Bentinck's in the absence of Lord William F——. They think that he will or may be disgusted with many different things, but much pleased with others. Talleyrand is better to-day, and seems to have been so ever since Madame de Talleyrand's death, about which he is said to have been more angry than anything else.

I have had a visit from Chabot—pleased with your letter, and I went with him to see Madame de Jarnac, who is very well, and sends you her love.

The box given by Madame Talleyrand to the *archevêque* for the Duchesse d'Esclaux contained bills or bonds for 380,000 francs. The *archevêque* is said to have summoned the witnesses of the transaction after the death, and instead of putting the box into Madame de Esclaux's hands, he put it on the table, when Prince Talleyrand's agent stepped in and took it. Fault is found at her being buried thirty-six hours after death, instead of waiting forty-eight. The Duc d'Esclaux (don't you remember seeing him and her at the breakfast at La Bretîche at Madame Durfort's?) is in Piedmont. Cradock's duel in a room, where he was wounded slightly in the arm, was about her some time ago.

It has been thawing, etc.

LETTER XXIV.

Paris, January 3rd, 1836.

Mr. Westmacott's son is making a valuable chimney-piece for Stafford House, with two statues ; it will please his father that he should have to do this.

We went yesterday evening, at eight o'clock, to the

réception aux Tuileries. We took Lady Elizabeth Howard,[*]
and went with the Schönbergs. We found all the rooms
and galleries full. The ladies all place themselves round
the walls, waiting for the progress of the royal family.
Ours advanced a considerable way, till they found Madame
de Dino, with whom they stayed, and the king soon reached
them. He is followed by the queen and the two princesses
and by Madame, and then the Duke of Nemours, who
all stop and say something to every lady, their ladies or
aide-de-camps ascertaining the names of all they did not
know.

The number was prodigious, and there will be another
to-morrow ; but we do not go again, but to a ball at the
Apponyis'. (While I think of it, allow me to ask whether
your spelling " partie *quarr*ée " is correct, and whether it be
not " *carr*ée " ? So I see the new Dictionnaire de l'Academie
says. I had thought it was as you have spelt it ; but I
suppose that we were wrong. Try T. Grenville or Lord
Clarendon about it.)

Ever most affectionately.

LETTER XXV.

January 4th.

Evelyn [†] has not got the measles ; but it seems to have
been a feverish cold, with sore throat and headache. She
has not suffered much, and her countenance has always
been cheerful. She is still rather feverish, and, having
some appearance of rash, we keep her in bed during this
cold weather. It is thawing to-day.

Madame de Flahault's second daughter seems seriously

----

[*] Afterwards wife of Hon. and Rev. Francis Grey, who died 1890.
[†] My sister, afterwards Lady Blantyre.

ill, having had a fever for nearly a fortnight, with too much blood going to the head.

LETTER XXVI.

Paris, January 8th, 1836.

Our principal worldly event has been the great ball at the Tuileries on the 6th, at which there were, I believe, full three thousand people.

The rooms are very well lighted, and the improvements made in the distribution, also a new gallery, made it a very magnificent affair.

The supper in the theatre, in which five tables are placed the whole length, at which ladies only sit down, is the finest sight of the sort (the men see it from the boxes) possible.

The king and queen, etc., sit in the Salle des Maréchaux during the dancing. It was very hot, and, I thought, tiresome enough after half-an-hour's seeing it.

The king at the reception asked Madame de Dino, " M. de Talleyrand, est-il content de moi?" and she said, "Sire, c'est son état naturel."

I went yesterday to the reception of M. Dupin at the Palais Bourbon—full of deputies, and I made acquaintance with Maréchal Macdonald, who looks very Scotch, though he mistook "Suth" for Sunderland, and said he had seen the bridge.

LETTER XXVII. ·

Chatsworth, September 19th, 1836.

Sneyd * is just going. He was amused at hearing of Sir C. Bagot † having been asked at some dinner who the

---

* Ralph Sneyd, of Keele Hall, near Trentham.
† Sir Charles Bagot, sometime British minister to the Netherlands, and died Governor-General of Canada.

Galitzins, lately in London, were, and saying it was difficult to distinguish them, as it was so common a name, like Smith here.

Sydney Smith was present, and said, "What are you saying about the name of Smith—*hé*, Charles?" "I was only explaining that Galitzin is the Russian for a Smith."

LETTER XXVIII.

October 21st, 1836.

This will probably await you in London, after, I hope, a good journey, and that you will have good accounts of your household. We have had high winds and wet weather, but were fortunate in a most perfect day, before yesterday, for a sort of triumphal entrance into the town of Gowran, a populous town on Lord Clifden's estate, to which Morpeth * and I and Trentham accompanied Lady Dover and her boys.

Harriet was unfortunately obliged to keep her room, and indeed her bed, with a bad feverish cold and cough. She improved very much yesterday—has had two good nights, and is now recovering, so that we shall all go to Bessborough, twenty-five miles from this, to-morrow.

We were met, three or four miles from Gowran, by several horsemen, some with flags and laurel branches to their horses, the number increasing, and near the town the crowd of inhabitants filling the roads and the streets, being over four or five thousand ; the cabins, cottages, and houses all decorated with boughs and ribbons.

Lady Dover proceeded, after we had driven through

---

* My mother's brother, afterwards Lord Carlisle, Lord-Lieutenant of Ireland.

the town, to a gentleman's house close by, and Morpeth and I and the boys went to the court-house. The priest carried Trentham part of the way on account of the press of the crowd. In the court-house he presented an address to me, alluding to the improvements in Sutherland, and hoping the same spirit might direct them here.

A gentleman addressed Morpeth. We answered, and then went to the agent's house—remarkably pretty, and he a gentlemanlike man, with a very pleasing wife.

They have just lost a daughter in a similar manner with Mr. Loch. (The English solicitor, Mr. Groom, whom we have appointed auditor, is an excellently well-disposed man, and anxious to do all that is right and can be done.)

A deputation came to present an address to Lady Dover, to which she read, in a very touching and admirable tone and manner, her answer. The last time she was there was with Lord Clifden and Dover, so that it was trying for her. But she does everything with great calm and spirit ; goes to the schools, to the dispensary, and inquires about the people ; has the clergy, both Protestant and Catholic, at dinner, and the others of the place. She is coming to Bessborough and Lord Clare's. We shall sleep a night between the two places, at the Duke of Devonshire's house, Lismore.

I enclose a request from the Birmingham School of Medicine to you concerning M——, and have two blue morocco-and-gilt reports for your acceptance from it.

I saw a very pretty place (Woodstock), belonging to Mr. and Lady Louisa Tighe,* where they do much good in their generation. They have no children. She is a Lennox, and seems pleasing and unaffected.

Ever most affectionately.

---

* Lady Louisa was a Lennox, daughter of the Duke of Richmond, who gave the celebrated ball on the eve of Waterloo.

Letter XXIX.

Phœnix Park, November 13th, 1836.

We returned yesterday from our expedition into Ulster, where we slept two nights at the Clanwilliams'. My dressing-room was that in which the ghost scene took place, an account of which I remember Lady Douglas, I think, once sending to you of Lord Tyrone appearing to his sister, Lady Beresford. There remains in it the chair in which she sat after seeing the ghost, until the account came of his death abroad at the time of her seeing it, and an old secrétaire chest of drawers, in each of which, small and great, are the marks in black of three fingers, which the ghost left as a proof of his having been there. Something like that, but of mysterious aspect, which Harriet declares is not any black paint, as I suggested. I think that Clanwilliam believes in the apparition.

Letter XXX.

Paris, Sunday, December 18th, 1836.

We arrived yesterday with Evelyn, and Talleyrand and the rest arrived all well to-day. Madame de Dino arrived yesterday. Talleyrand has been for about a week in Paris, and is said to be remarkably well and *rajeuni*. Madame de Lieven came to see Harriet to-day, and is remarkably well.

The disappointment in the failure in Africa is great for the king and ministry, just before the opening of the Chambers, when they wish to have something to boast of.

The country between Calais and this is much flooded, and the Seine has overflowed, and prevents Madame

Appony from having a *soirée* to-morrow. I will send your letter to Debare. A catalogue which he had sent to me in London has been sent back here to me to-day, and in it the enclosed for you, showing the arms, which you already know.

Mr. Guthrie's advice about amusing yourself, and not plaguing yourself, seems to me very good.

Ever most affectionately.

LETTER XXXI.

Monday, 1836.

Harriet is prevented from dining at the Granvilles'* by a headache. Unlucky, as it is a dinner for her of all her friends — Princess Schönberg, Madame de Lieven, etc. Trentham is to come to dessert, as it is his birthday.

I see in the newspaper the death of poor Princess Radzivil, who was always so very kind to me, and was an excellent, clever, and agreeable person. She had suffered much from the deaths of her children and family misfortunes. She was a most estimable person.

LETTER XXXII.

Paris, December 28th, 1836.

Encore un attentat! What a state of wretched anxiety for the king and queen and family! It made the *séance royal* extremely interesting yesterday. We were at it. Lady Granville did not go, and Harriet had her ticket and went, as last year, with Princess Schönberg, with whom she

* Lord Granville was ambassador to France, and was uncle to the writer. Lady Granville was a sister of the then Duke of Devonshire, and the aunt of the Duchess of Sutherland.

enjoys talking ; and as one goes at eleven, and the king
does not come till one, it is well to be in good company for
those two hours.. I had an excellent place in another
tribune.

The queen and princesses arrived a little before one.
The king did not arrive at the expected time. A French-
man in our tribune repeatedly said, " Soyez sur messieurs
qu'il y est quelquechose arrivée." We saw M. Dupin call
out Montalivet, and the latter resume his place with a very
grave and anxious look. Then a low communication
among the peers and deputies, and in our tribune, which
was on a level with the Chambre, we were told, " Qu'on
avait tiré sur le Roi, que personne n'était frappé," and that
the assassin was arrested. Just after this the *cortége* began
to enter, and the king was received with a general shout of
" Vive le Roi ! " several times repeated ; he stopped on the
steps of his throne to bow and make signs of thanks, and
the cries " Vive le Roi ! " and " Vive la Reine ! " (who had
been informed of what had happened, and had been affected
and crying, but continued in her place) were long continued.

The king read his speech with much firmness till he
came to the mention of the *attentat* of Alibeau, which
occasioned a renewal of the " Vive le Roi ! " and his voice
was afterwards less strong. The ceremony was over before
two. The Chambers went to the Tuileries to the king. The
Diplomatic Tribune did not hear of the event till they
came out, and, to my surprise, as I was waiting in the
corridor for Harriet, when they passed me I found them
ignorant, and was the first to tell them.

They thought something must have happened from the
unusual reception of the king, but did not know what.

I thought that the Duke of Orleans seemed to hold his
hand to his face a great part of the time ; and we afterwards found that the broken glass of the carriage window

had cut his ear and face, so as to make it bleed, and, I believe, scratched the Duc de Nemours' also. It was a wonderful escape, as the king's head was at the window, bowing.

After we had come home, Harriet and I walked to Madame de Lieven's to hear more, and found that she had not yet heard of it.

I dined at Duchatel's, the Minister of Finance, when the ambassadors and some ministers, etc., also dined, and afterwards went with Granville to the Tuileries, where people were crowding to offer their respects, as we did. The king said that the man had declared that he had sworn to kill him since 1830.

We then went to M. Molé's reception, it being his night, and also to Montalivet's; and then Harriet and I visited the Duchesse de Poix, and finished the evening at a party at Madame de Flahault's.

To-night we have the order for the king's box, for the French Opera, and we are going to take the children. There is much snow in the streets, and yesterday and to-day there have been several sledges about.

We dine with Talleyrand on Saturday. I saw Madame de Dino last night; very well. We went for our first visit to the Tuileries on Friday last. They inquired very kindly after you.

LETTER XXXIII.

December 30th.

I have little to add. We have had no English news for a longer time than I believe ever was the case before. They have taken advantage of the suspense to imagine a report of the death of the King of England.

P

I have had a letter from P. Radzivil, which I am so pleased with that I have copied it for you.*

We have the royal box at the French Opera again, and take Evelyn, who did not go to the last opera, which the others enjoyed extremely.   Very cold.

Ever affectionately.

Extract of a letter from Paris, January 6th, 1837.

We went to the reception at the Tuileries on Tuesday. The number of people there was very great, and the king and queen must have been heartily tired before they had spoken to every one. We dined with Count Pahlen on Wednesday. Madame de Dino looked very handsome in a rich turban. Talleyrand seems very well; he was amused before dinner *chez lui* at our remarking that all of us who happened to be in a group in the drawing-room had met on former occasions before the revolution—namely, Mr. Cutler Ferguson, Montron, Granville, himself, and me.

LETTER XXXIV.

Paris, Monday, January 9th, 1837.

We are going on very well here.   Harriet is gone with Lord Granville to see the balloon mount; after which to the

---

* "Berlin, December 17th, 1836.—It has pleased God to call my mother from this life. She died on the 7th of this month, after an illness of seven days, surrounded by us, and without long sufferings. God grant us to be so well prepared for a better life when He shall call upon us to leave this. Your Grace has admired too faithfully the elevated mind and the amiable qualities of the deceased to be a stranger to our grief.   You will feel it deeply with us. I feel obliged to express these sentiments to your Grace in my name, and in the name of my brother and sister, to tell you that my mother constantly con-sidered you as a dear friend.   Believe me, your Grace's obedient servant, W. PRINCE RADZIVIL."

Chambre des Pairs, where the Duc de Broglie and Montalivet are expected to speak on the address ; after which we
dine at the Tuileries, where many English are to dine
to-day ; after which Madame Appony's ball, being the first
given this year.

On Saturday Harriet dined at the Granvilles' for a
Scotch and English dinner of Cumming Gordons, Ran-
furleys, etc. I dined at a great man dinner at the Préfet
de la Seine ; sat by old Soult, who has grown much
thinner and older, and looks more respectable for it, and by
the Duc Decazes, who is extremely civil about tickets for
the Chambre des Pairs, of which he is Grand Chamberlan.

Yesterday we dined out, and afterwards went to three
soirées, including Madame de la Briche's, whose Sunday
evening is said to have continued since before the revolution.

Sosthène de la Rochefoucauld has been publishing his
correspondence with Madame de Cayla, in spite of her
daughter, Madame de Craon, and her own remonstrances.
I mention it as surpassing Lord Wharncliffe's indiscretion.

LETTER XXXV.

Monday night.

I have opened my letter, after dining at the Tuileries,
to say that nothing could be more kind and civil. A very
large dinner. They made us the chief guests, I taking
the queen, and the king taking Harriet. We have just
returned. Many kind inquiries after you. The debate
in the Chambre des Pairs was interesting. The Duc de
Broglie speaks very well, easily, and clearly ; M. de Molé
well also, and the Duc de Noailles very fairly.

The other two speeches of the Marquis de Brézé and

of M. Boissy d'Anglas were read and tiresome ; and then we were obliged to come away for the dinner.

Harriet saw the balloon ascend and strike against a chimney ; rather alarming, but not fatal.

Ever most affectionately.

LETTER XXXVI.

Paris, Sunday night, January 15th, 1837.

If I do not say something to-night, I know that I shall not have time to-morrow, as the Chambre des Députés begins—at least, it is necessary to go there to get a place— at ten o'clock, and Guizot and Berryer are both expected to speak, and it will last till near dinner-time, when Molé and a large party are to dine at the Granvilles'. In the Tribune Diplomatique in the Chambre, for which we have tickets, there are always several of one's acquaintance, and great expectation and agitation makes it entertaining. Thiers made a long clever speech yesterday. The Duc de Broglie made a very good one in the Chambre des Pairs the other day, telling us, what few seemed to know, about the Salic law not having been ever established in Spain ; that the ladies were only made to give way to males by the Pragmatic Sanction, which had been done away with in modern times, not by Ferdinand, who did not leave his daughter the crown by his will, but appointed the regency by it ; that his daughter's right had been previously acknow- ledged and undoubted.

LETTER XXXVII.

Paris, January 19th, 1837.

We took all the children yesterday evening to Madame Appony's to see a ventriloquist act, very amusingly, three different parts, in our old dining-room, and to hear some Tyrolese sing in the old drawing-room. I felt pleasure in seeing them amused in our old habitation, and it was a sort of coincidence. The Duc de Laval * told Harriet that she was like Niobe with her children, which idea pleased him exceedingly.

The debates in the Chambre des Députés have been very interesting, and have given an opportunity of hearing all the best speeches—Thiers, Berryer, and Guizot.

LETTER XXXVIII.

Friday night, January 20th.

We have been to pay our respects at the Tuileries, and were there when the Chambre des Députés were presenting their address in the next room to the king. We heard the "Vive le Roi!" at the end of his answer, and he brought them all in to make their bows to the queen, between whom and Madame, Harriet was sitting at the time, so she saw them all proceed round the table, and round the table and out. The king seemed in good spirits, and said to me that the majority had been a good one. We then also came away.

The Strasburg conspirators are acquitted, owing to the principal having been let off!

There is to be a ball for four thousand at the Tuileries on Wednesday. Many think it a risk for the king, as people can get in in disguise. What a state to be in!

Ever most affectionately.

* The Duc de Laval was French ambassador in London in the last days of the reign of Charles X.

LETTER XXXIX.

Paris, Sunday, February 12th, 1837.

Poor M. de Guizot, the Ministre d'Instruction, has an only son, a pleasing young man about twenty, dying slowly of a decline. He sleeps well and eats well, but still is dying; and M. Guizot, with all the cares of a minister, the chief *soutien* of his Government, is in great affliction about his son—passes much of the night with him, and, they say, cannot bear to be asked about him.

We are beginning to see some people again—Madame de Lieven, etc. She said that some time ago they were talking at Talleyrand's of parrots, and of their living to an old age. Talleyrand said, "Oh, they, the parrots, lived to be very old ; j'en ai vus même qui radottent."

I enclose an *éloge* of M. Van Praet, the *conservateur* of the Bibliothèque Royale, much regretted here. Perhaps Mr. Grenville would like to have it.

LETTER XL.

Paris, February 24th, 1837.

I have some idea of buying Madame Le Brun's original portrait of the Queen Marie Antoinette, for which she sat, and from which Madame Le Brun painted the others. It is not full length. I think its being the original makes it very interesting. Madame Le Brun is very old, looking at herself in the glass while she is talking, with several of her pictures on her walls—the King of Poland, Madame de Mierfeldt, the Comte de Vaudreuil, Empress of Russia, herself, etc.

LETTER XLI.

Paris, March 17th, 1837.

When the king was looking at and going over the Opera House at Versailles the other day, some one picked up a piece of paper, rolled up, from a crevice in the floor, and found it to be a *billet d'entrée* for the Opera for the year 1778, that had been there dropped, and had remained undisturbed all the eventful time since.

The dinner in the Gallery of Versailles is to exceed one thousand *couverts*. I hope there will appear no writing on the wall. I have been waiting for the cheap Paris edition of Lord Wharncliffe's "Lady M. W. Montagu's Letters," and have therefore not read them.

There is a general impression that things are going ill here. These money questions have had a bad effect, and people are inclined to be discontented and to want confidence.

Madame de Jarnac says the Archbishop of Paris, in protesting against having the site of the *archevêché* made a public garden (in exchange for which they had offered him an hotel in the Rue de Bourbon), wishes to make *de l'embarras*. Delpêche knows of no likeness of Madame des Ursins. I have not any further intelligence from Madame de Dino about her.

Lord Haddo goes with Sir C. Vaughan to Constantinople on Saturday.

The *fonderies* in bronze are wonderful here ; such a number of them, and entertaining people, so fond of their work. Did I tell you that Trentham, much to his annoyance, has been sitting for a bust, and that it is to be a statue in a Highland costume as large as himself, so must take care

not to have it like those before tobacconists' shops, taking a pinch of snuff?

This is one, the last, of Lady Granville's Fridays. Her Royal Highness Madame l'Électrice de Bavière, wife of a Comte d'Arcot in Bavaria, is to be a feature of it.

LETTER XLII,

Paris, March 24th, 1837.

We had a clear, cold night on Tuesday for our astronomical visit to the Observatory. M. Arago was very communicative, and as he is a man one often hears of, it is agreeable to have known him.

It was a full moon, and therefore not good for astronomizing. We saw Jupiter with his band and fiery mass, and a double star, and heard that though light travels so quickly, it is supposed to require thirty years to come to us from some of the stars.

Arago made an entertaining speech in the Chambre de Députés yesterday in favour of teaching sciences in preference to literature; the cause of the latter being taken up by Lamartine, with whom Harriet has made a friendship.

Other more closely interesting subjects to the king will come on soon. The affair of the *apanages* has had a very bad effect generally.

The African business is also very interesting here. General Claussel is brought over the coals in a way one would not like any friend of one's own to be, and his defence in the shape of his published "Explication" seems very indiscreet and in bad taste. As one does not care for any concerned, and has no high opinion of any (it is said that those who preceded Claussel were as bad), we may let them *s'arranger* as they can, and shrug our shoulders about it.

I imagine that you do this about Spanish affairs also. What I am more, and very much, concerned about is Horseburgh's * death, as I fear he will be a very serious loss to you ; and at the time of a new factor being also required for the other part of that extensive and remote district, requiring management and surveillance as it does, such a loss is much to be regretted.

We are buying some bronzes for the garden of Trentham, and some things for Stafford House. The bronze-founders here are very engaging people, and I suppose that such establishments as exist here are not to be found elsewhere.

It is quite a new set of people—at least, that I had not found before—chiefly in the neighbourhood of the Père la Chaise, and some in the Marais.

Ever most affectionately.

LETTER XLIII.

Paris, April 3rd, 1837.

M. Thiers (the late and probably future minister), who is occupied in the midst of his French politics with a History of Florence and the Medicis, suggested to Harriet that one could have nothing more rare and admirable than the gates of the Baptistery of Florence, by Ghiberti, which Michael Angelo used to say were fit to be the gates of Paradise ; and that the Government here had the plaster casts of them, and that he had put some of the casts as bas-reliefs in his library, which he yesterday took us to see, and that he could enable us to have them cast

* Factor of the Sutherland estates.

here in bronze if we liked. This would be tempting; but I do not think that we have any very good place for it. The door itself would be near nineteen feet high.

I think it might have not a bad effect at the north end of the gallery, to be a false door. The bas-relief is only for one side, and it would look as if it led to something very extraordinary. But it would be a disappointment, and altogether, perhaps, too much of an extravagance.

I have been to take another good view of the Duchesse de Berry's pictures, which are to be sold by auction, which begins to-morrow and lasts three days, and may be expected to be had for more reasonable prices than were asked in London.

I should like a Panini, a Wynants, a Moucheron, and a Vernet—all very pleasing; so shall see.

Madame de Jarnac has a loss with Madame de Bel [illegible] whom Chabot says you will remember, a great friend of the Comte Etienne. Here is an extract from a *feuilleton* in the *Journal des Debats* of to-day to fill up my letter, giving an account of a concert for the relief of Italian refugees: "Dans cette foule brillante etoient confondus, dans la même admiration et dans la même sympathie M. et Madame Appony, Madame la Duchesse de Sutherland, ce beau portrait de Lawrence, mais un portrait qui marche, qui sourit, qui tend la main à toute les infortunes; M. Thiers, M. Berryer, Madame de Mouchy."

I think if you were here you would encourage our extravagances in the fine arts, and they are really good things that I have been buying.

Ever most affectionately.

END OF PART V.

PART VI.

LETTER I.

Saturday, July 15th, 1837.*

We dined at Buckingham Palace. Only Lord Melbourne, the John Russells, Charlemonts, and maids of honour, and equerry, and lord and groom in waiting.

I took in the Duchess of Kent, and was between her and the queen.

The duke desired me to say many things to you, and I told the queen of your regret at being obliged to go before the Drawing-Room.

She was in very good spirits and agreeable. After dinner we went upstairs to the pink stucco room.

The Duchess of Kent had a rubber. The queen sat on a sofa with Harriet and the Princess de Leiningen,† and Lord Melbourne and I at the table ; and she conversed very easily, seemed to like to talk to Lord Melbourne about a petition from the Quakers, and sensible sort of talk.

I have been to-day with Lord Conyngham to Windsor to see the Crown jewels there, and we brought up what we thought would be most interesting for the queen to have at present—collars, and badges of orders, etc.

July 17th, 1837.

I imagine that there is an end of franking, but I shall be glad to pay for a good letter from you from Dunrobin

* Three weeks after the accession of the young queen. Lord Melbourne was Prime Minister, and Lord John Russell Home Secretary.

† Wife of the Duchess of Kent's son by her first husband.

with the account of your arrival.   Meanwhile, I must tell you
that the queen has delighted every one at the prorogation
to-day by the manner of her delivering her speech.

I think it not possible to imagine a more delightful
voice and emphasis, so clear, sweet, gentle, and harmonious,
and with such presence of mind and composure, that it was
really as perfect as possible.   And she also looked very
well, with her circlet of diamonds and her robes and
perfect gravity, and filled the throne very gracefully—no
nervousness.

Harriet and Lord Albemarle went with her in the
coach, and she was very cheerful, and all that could be
wished, all the time.

The day was fine ; all the world out, and the reception
throughout enthusiastic.

The Duchess of Kent had preceded her, and sat on the
woolsack.

The speech itself was much approved by the Tories.
Lord Roden said he never heard a better ; in short, it has
been extremely satisfactory.

LETTER II.

London, July 29th, 1837.

Lady George Grey will have heard that Lady Durham is
one of the Ladies of the Bedchamber.   There was a concert after a dinner at which we dined at the palace last night.
Not a large company ; very fine music, but very long ; but
it was not hot, and I got into the gallery during all the
second act, where it was pleasant walking and looking at
the pictures.

There are some reforms at court that you will approve
of.   No question about precedence with envoys and

diplomats (not ambassadors), as there used to be at Brighton.

Sir Fred. Watson, and therefore, I suppose, all others of no higher grade, dine at some other table, and only appear after dinner. The queen seems to attend to details, and to wish to have all in order and right, and to be very decided.

The Duke of Sussex* and Princess Sophia dined yesterday. Princess Sophia preceded the Duchess of Kent. Sir J. Conroy is never seen or heard of. What a change for him and disappointment it must be!

There is a young Danish prince come over for a few days, rather genteel, only nineteen. I suppose he has been sent to see and to be seen, but I should not think with any chance.

Madame de Lieven meant to have left us to-day, but being invited to the concert last night, she will now stay till Tuesday. We should have thought her a loss if we had to stay much longer, as her visit has been very agreeable to us all, including the children, who are very fond of her and of her niece, who returns to Paris.

What an odd thing for Lady Westminster to think of buying the Nassac and other enormous diamonds for above £21,000!

LETTER III.

London, August 8th, 1837.

I suppose that it is right for me to write to wish you joy of my birthday and Evelyn's.†

I am glad that your elections are over. The queen has wished Harriet to stay two days longer on account of the King of Wurtemburg coming (who is particularly

* The Queen's favourite uncle.

† My parents' second daughter, born in 1826, afterwards Lady Blantyre.

recommended to us by Elizabeth). We are to dine on Thursday, when he is expected, and therefore shall not be able to go till the 14th, and then I cannot have the ploughing-match at Trentham till the end of next week, or leave it till the following. This will make it the end of August before we can be at Dunrobin, but it is better to get the ploughing-match over now, than to have to hurry back for it.

The Robert Grosvenors * are going to Ems directly. I fear that his health is in a very bad state; that she is much alarmed about him.

I hope that the Grosvenors have relieved you from all anxiety about their voyage by their arrival. It was certainly too windy on the day they left London, but we hoped that somehow they would not feel it so much; but I think the land is best, however long, and not to imagine one need be in a violent hurry. We had a very successful expedition to Salthill on Friday and Saturday. We saw all the castle, and had the queen's pony-carriages (for the Mistress of the Robes) to drive over all the Park, and went on the Virginia Water. We had some heavy showers, but with fine intervals. We slept at Salthill, and on Saturday walked over the gardens at Dropmore (Lady Grenville and Mr. Grenville had gone in the morning to Windsor). We then drove through Burnham Beeches, with which, and the quantity of juniper, we were delighted.

Interrupted by a visit from Rogers, who says all the poets are in town. Wordsworth came yesterday from Italy. The Hollands have gone by slow *journées* to Dover. The Carlisles left this for Castle Howard yesterday. The Harrowbys are going to Wilton. Love to Eliz.

Ever most affectionately.

* Lord Ebury and Lady Ebury.

The elections seem to leave numbers much as they were, with the improvement of being rid of Mr. Roebuck. Here is Sneyd going to Paris soon, but to Wilton first.

LETTER IV.

Lilleshall, August 15th, 1837.

We left London about three yesterday, and have had fine summer weather for the journey, and a beautiful moon, but, on account of the children, could not avail ourselves of it, as we might otherwise have done. We dined at Buckingham Palace on Friday, when I again sat by Princess Sophia,* so that we have become very intimate. The King of Wurtemburg and a large party dined on that day. The queen invited us for Sunday, our last day. She has not large dinners on Sunday, and this was chiefly household, Lord Portman and I being the only strangers. Lady Portman was in waiting. Surrey dined, but, as the Duke of Argyll was there, he had not to officiate at the end of the table, as he would do in the absence of the Lord Steward ; but he is very properly desirous of having everything in good order, and wishes the household always to come to dinner, etc., in their *levée* uniform, and he came to suggest to Harriet that she should suggest this to the queen (it being in neither of their departments), and he since found that all the household are very much against it, so that is not to be done.

Poor Princess Elizabeth has had a fall in her library at Homburg over the carpet, which brought them all into the room in a great alarm. She is not much hurt, only her hands bruised, and of course some difficulty in getting up again.

* Princess Sophia and Princess Elizabeth were daughters of George III., and aunts of the queen.

Q

The queen was very kind, full of regret at losing Harriet, and, if not inconvenient, hoping to have her for the dinner at Guildhall on the 9th of November.

16th.

Another delightful day of fine weather. We are going on to Trentham, where we shall have the ploughing-match on Friday, after which I shall write to Mr. Loch, which I have not done for some time since or during his election.

Ever affectionately.

LETTER V.

From my Mother to the Duchess Countess.

Trentham, August 25th, 1837.

DEAREST DUCHESS,

I am much obliged to you for your letter and the inclosure intended for me. I am happy in having began our journey towards you, and sorry not to be with you for the first arrival of the Francises * and children. I long to see the addition to the house, and the monument, of which I have formed a high idea.

My father has not been unwell, except a little gout and rheumatism. I was spared all anxiety from these evil reports, but several persons were much frightened. I have never been late in my royal attendance. I have enjoyed seeing the queen *de si près*, and admire much what I have observed.

This place is in beautiful country, and they have

* Lord Francis Egerton (afterwards Lord Ellesmere) and his wife. Writing of Lord Francis a few months later, Mr. Disraeli said, " Lord Francis Egerton spoke with all the effect which a man of considerable talent and highly cultivated mind, backed by the highest rank and £60,000 a year, would naturally command."

improved and made gardens with great taste and judgment.

The Burlingtons * returned from Bolton the same day
that we arrived, where they have had good shooting.
Morpeth was there, enjoying himself after his great fatigues.

Stafford is looking thin, and I look forward with
pleasure to the breezes of Dunrobin.

> Believe me, my dearest duchess,
> > Yours ever affectionately,
> > > HARRIET SUTHERLAND.

LETTER VI.

Windsor Castle, December 31st, 1837.

The year ends with the finest weather, and I hope the
next will begin as well, and I wish you all other possible
good wishes for it.

As we hope to see you at dinner, I need not say much.
Our visit here has been very agreeable. Harriet drove out
with the queen the first day, and on the second, when the
Cambridges were here and the queen drove with them, we
followed in other carriages.

Yesterday the queen and Duchess of Kent rode, and a
large party. I had a very good pleasant horse and rode
by them; Harriet and Lady Mulgrave followed in a
pony-carriage. The Duchess of Cambridge made an
agreeable variety in the society. She fell to my care
the two dinners she had here. On the other days I have

---

* Lord Burlington was the present (1890) Duke of Devonshire. Lady
Burlington was my mother's younger sister, who died in 1840, eighteen years
before her husband succeeded his cousin in the dukedom. Morpeth was my
mother's eldest brother, who as Lord Carlisle was twice Viceroy of Ireland.
At this period he was chief secretary to the Lord-Lieutenant, Lord Mulgrave
(created Marquis of Normanby the next year), whose wife is mentioned below.

the honour of taking the queen, so I hope to be able to do so properly for you to-morrow.

Ever most affectionately.

LETTER VII.

Bowood, January 10th, 1838.

T. Moore began singing yesterday, and began with two melancholy songs, and in the second was seized with hysterics, crying, so that he was obliged to run out of the room. He soon recovered and returned, and sang more lively airs very prettily. It was probably seeing poor Lady Kerry,* and thinking of a daughter that he lost, that together upset him at the time. The grounds here are very pretty, with many fine evergreens and a pretty piece of water. Barry improved the house very essentially by adding a little passage from one part to the other.

Ever affectionately. .

LETTER VIII.

Genoa, October 6th, 1838.†

' We have had a delightful drive to-day by the seashore to the west (very like the sea at Dunrobin), and walks in the gardens of the Villas Doria, Lonedrin, etc. We arrived the day before yesterday in good time from Alessandria, had a good journey from Turin, whence I wrote to you. We have seen a good deal of the principal sights of Genoa and neighbourhood yesterday and to-day, and shall finish

---

* Lord Kerry, the eldest son of Lord Lansdowne, the owner of Bowood, had died in 1836, at the age of twenty-five, within two years of his marriage with Lady A. Ponsonby.

† There is some mistake about the date of this letter, but it is not of importance, and I insert it here.   . .

to-morrow and proceed by short journeys by the beautiful
coast road to Lucca, which we shall reach in four days
on Sunday. It was a great delight to receive yesterday evening your letter of the 26th from London. I
shall not fail to give your presents as you desire on
Stafford's birthday, which will make all concerned very
happy, and it is very kind in you to have thought of it.
The Brignoles came from their *villégiature* at Voltri to-
day for the court, which has made its entry from Turin.
They pass a month here, where they do not seem to
be much cared for. The king has given a very fine
palace lately, that of the queen-dowager, to the Jesuits, of
whom one sees many walking about, always in pairs (not
being allowed to walk out singly). There are also many
of other orders, and monks. The king is, I believe, devout.

We found Turin a finer town than we expected, and
I think are both perhaps rather disappointed in this, of
which one has always heard so much. What I remember
struck me before is still much the case here—that the
palaces, which originally looked splendid when first painted
and in good order, look now very different, out of order
and *dégradés*, and the architecture is not exemplary of
any, and the approaches to the hotels are often very bad,
and we are ill-lodged, and therefore not favourably prejudiced. We dine to-morrow with the Brignoles.* I
believe their collection of pictures is as fine as any here.
Steamboats smoke in the harbour, and bring a recollection
of English coal, which rather surprises one. Yesterday
was cold enough for it. This has been a delightful speci-
men of our best Dunrobin summer weather. Quantities
of flowery broom in the Doria gardens. I was near

* This family became connected with the Leveson-Gowers. The only
child of Emeric, Duc de Dalberg, by his wife Pellina, daughter of the
Marquis Brignole Sale, married as her second husband, in 1840, Lord
Leveson, now second Lord Granville.

giving way to sentiment, and enclosing a bunch of it ; **but**
I am not sure that you are sentimental enough to warrant
such an attention. If you are, you must be pleased and
satisfied with the intention.

The Doria houses in town and country here are
most terribly out of repair (as Mdlle. Moldenhauer was
shocked to find), and I shall have to state this to Lady
Shrewsbury. I expected to get out of Genoa without
being guilty of any extravagance, and I really think that
Trentham is as pretty in decoration as any house we have
seen. Mr. Gloag begins to be impatient to get to Rome,
as he says that three ladies are expecting his assistance as
accoucheur about the 13th. He is rather an original,
but I think we like him, and so shall be sorry to lose him
at Florence. But there is very good English and Scotch
advice there in case of need. Elizabeth was quite wrong
in not thinking it very desirable to have advice with one,
and he has been most useful. The Brignoles interrupted
my writing by an evening visit, full of civilities, and
desire compliments to you. We dine with them to-morrow
and proceed next day.

Ever most affectionately.

LETTER IX.

Windsor, October 8th, 1838.

I was obliged to interrupt my letter to see Sir A. Macdonald, to whom, by a strange coincidence, I had written
yesterday ; but not knowing in what part of the world he
might be, my letter was on the table, sealed and ready for
him, with good advice in it, and a present of the Duke of
Wellington's "Despatches," which is an admirable work,
most extremely interesting for any one, and particularly, of

course, for a military man ; and if he reads it, it cannot
fail to be of use to him, and if he does not become en-
grossed with it, I have told him he may be sure that he
is not good for anything.   I don't know if that assurance
will have any good effect.

Letter X.

Windsor Castle, October 9th, 1838.

I find that a messenger goes at three o'clock, so I will
write a line or two for him.

We found nearly all the Cabinet ministers here, and
they had all been of the queen's riding party yesterday.
The Duchess of Kent thinks H. B. would have made something of their party on horseback.   Princess Augusta, with
Miss Hope Johnstone, dined.

The queen seems very well.   Lady Lyttelton is in
waiting, and a very good addition to a court party.   The
queen had a fall one day, but a gentle one.   Sir G. Quen-
tin contrived to break it for her, and she did not mind it
at all.

The Duchess of Kent also had one, and rather hurt her
arm, but she continues to ride too.   Lady May Stafford
is at her post.   Constance * and Victoria are with her,
Constance thinking Victoria "a very little thing to come
to Windsor."

Letter XI.

Windsor Castle, October 9th, 1838.

Among other people here we have found Lord Ux-.
bridge, very civil and obliging, which has made me recollect

---

* The late Duchess of Westminster; her little sister, Lady Victoria
Gower, died the following year, 1839.

old occurrences which I have read of in letters of the former Lords Uxbridge *tempore* George III. (Have you read Brougham's bitter observations in the *Edinburgh Review* concerning him, George III.?) There is nothing extraordinary in the circumstance of Lord Uxbridge's grandson being here now, in the reign of the granddaughter of George III., and of my meeting him here; but somehow it seems an improvement, and I prefer him to his grandfather, and pleasanter to be all well together, though no one knows how long it may be so.

Our ride to-day was very agreeable. We were out till six o'clock, most of the time in the Forest, in which the green miles seem endless and most varied and charming. I had a good steady horse, which kept by the queen's side very dutifully and properly, and we had no accidents.

The Duchess of Kent shortened her ride by taking to the carriage, and got home about half an hour before us.

Harriet drove with Lady Lyttelton.

LETTER XII.

October 19th (Friday), 1838.

Very much relieved on arriving at Vale Royal to receive your letter from Calais. The weather has been so stormy I felt very uneasy; Mr. Grenville also, who partook in the good news, but he was not up to all my regrets and lamentations at the damage done by a hurricane at Dunrobin on the 12th. The scaffolding of the statue carried up into the air (the statue not damaged), trees innumerable; in short, Loch and Mrs. Loch describe it as frightful. I went to Vale Royal, a fine and curious house; then here yesterday, very comfortable, and luckily a fine day after much bad weather; and Lord Harrowby and I are just returning from passing the morning at Trentham. I thought the statue admirable, and the alterations and improvements equally so. It is already beautiful, even in its unfinished state. The garden, terraces, etc., in the most perfect old French taste; the fountains and the approach to the house perfect. The effect of the tower, also, the Stanfield's, very pretty, but as you have seen it so lately I need not recapitulate. Mrs. Kirke took great care of us, and Penson, Wooley, and Mutchin, with Mr. Lewis, were very kind in their reception of us, and showed us everything *con amore* and in detail. I ought not to omit Mr. Webster. It was really very gratifying to see the young plantations much grown. Everything looked well, and we were much pleased with some hours which we passed there. Mrs. Kirke had, in fact, prepared a good dinner for us. This is the summary of what we did, and we thought ourselves very fortunate in our day. Barsly arrives there to-night to take care of me from Stafford on Monday, when I propose to be in London at night by the railway, by which I have successfully performed the most part of my journeys. Francis goes to town on Tuesday to send his boy off by steam to Gibraltar, and so on to Italy. I have shown my correspondence with D—— to Mr. Grenville, who admires it, and says I could not in reason do otherwise; Lord Stanley also, and Lord Harrowby, who is much amused by it. You see if I had not made Achintool a primary matter, and it is of importance, he might not have proposed giving it up; so it is well I did, and I will stick to every word I say, which has been in a manner foretold already in the newspapers.

LETTER XIII.

Paris, Friday, October 23rd, 1838.

We arrived this evening, having slept at Abbeville and Beauvais.

The children were much pleased with having seen the cathedrals of Abbeville and Beauvais and the church of St. Denis.

Our house here has some good rooms, very ill distributed, so that it is not very easy to make our arrangements very comfortable ; but that does not signify, as " we are but sojourners here."

We had fine weather for our journey, and France was seen to advantage.

I think the woods seem to have improved much since we were last here, seven years ago, and the men were busy ploughing, etc.

LETTER XIV.

Lyons, October 26th, 1838.

I write a line from hence, as the last opportunity before we leave France, to say that our journey has been prosperous.

We do not make very long days in general, as we try not to travel in the dark.

We yesterday stayed at Macon to make a visit to M. de Lamartine,* who lives fifteen miles from it, in a pretty

* Lamartine at this period was forty-eight years old, and at the height of his fame. Eight years previously, a few months before the Revolution of July, he had become a member of the French academy. His "Voyage en Orient," referred to below, was made in 1833, and during his absence from France he was elected deputy for Dunkerque, thus commencing his political

mountainous country, like part of the Highlands; but he has also a place nearer Macon, with fine vineyards. He is a *seigneur*, with three *châteaux;* the one we visited you would have been much pleased with—an old castle with towers, with thick walls, irregular stairs ; and they seem to live very comfortably and socially. We met two carriages of people coming from him, who had been dining early with him. We drove in a little carriage, taking Elizabeth with us, and were very much pressed to stay, rooms being prepared ; and Harriet was afraid she would have been obliged to have stayed the night without clothes or preparation, as our horses had knocked up in going ; but we contrived to return, very much pleased with our visit.

He is very agreeable. She was English, and travelled with him on horseback through Asia and Turkey, and would, therefore, think nothing of passing a night without preparation. But we travel more carefully.

We hope to sleep at Echelles to-night. Harriet sends her kindest love. Elizabeth is delighted with the journey, and we get on very well.

Ever most affectionately.

Letter XV.

October 26th, 1838.

I must write a few words to say how glad I was to receive yours from Calais, and two from Paris, and how much my thoughts go with you and my wishes.

I have to beg that on Stafford's birthday you will distribute the following sum from me :—to Stafford him-

tour. He was born on the eve of the French Revolution, in a small house in the town of Macon, but at this period he was inhabiting the Château de St. Point.

self three sequins, Caroline three, Evelyn four, Elizabeth five, and George Egerton five.* I will repay you in London. George E—— has just sailed from Falmouth, which makes us *look after* these winds. He will probably touch at Tangiers, as Mr. Robert Hay, who is fortunately in the same vessel, means to touch there, and will afterwards proceed to Italy. I made a very successful railway journey from Stafford here in nine hours, in my own carriage, on the 22nd, and saw a blazing fire at Harrow in passing, which has consumed Dr. Drury's old house and those of the principal masters, owing to one of those stoves I so much dread. By-the-by, I fear you will have some plague with the new flues at Trentham, which, they say, smoke abominably. I am more and more pleased with my riddance of D——. He was always doing everything troublesome and hostile, receiving favours, pretending he meant nothing; in short, most impertinent. Jealous of us in the extreme—as if there were common sense in that— nig-nagging, vain-glorious, and pompous; and, if I am "morosely just and monstrously severe," I render an essential service to my family and myself in *taking any opportunity* to give him a touch of the cat's paw, which he well deserves. With all that, he is the best adversary Loch can have, as he will oppose him by noise, and not with the heavy purse of another who once thought of it. Great talks here of politics; but you are more likely than I to hear it all. I forgot to say that my correspondence with D—— was approved much by Mr. Grenville.

I am making a *potager* for myself on Barsley's ground at Hammersmith, merely for vegetables and fruit, and a

---

* Lord Stafford, referred to in previous letters as Trentham, third Duke of Sutherland; Lady Caroline, afterwards Duchess of Leinster, Lady Evelyn, afterwards Lady Blantyre, and Lady Elizabeth, afterwards Duchess of Argyle, the children of the writer; George Egerton, afterwards second Earl of Ellesmere, his nephew.

very small grape-house, which is to have a plant of the Black Prince grape from you at Trentham.

I went the day after I arrived to Westhill, and found Frederick much strengthened and improved, and very amiable. Constance extremely entertaining. I cannot conceive where she gets all her words and ideas. She is very clever. Victoria is, I think, extremely pretty and very good. I go there again this morning, and I shall bring them to town to breakfast, etc., on the 11th of November, Frederick's birthday, the idea of which seems to give satisfaction. There are some people in town. I dine to-day with Lady Davy, to meet Lord Gage, etc. B—— says that Mr. Bucknal is the happiest man in the world. Char. comes to make me a visit next week ; Lord William Bentinck takes Polly. Lord Henry Bentinck wants to have the Reay Forest ; he might as well ask me to let Dunrobin to him. Loch's girl is recovering, and he was to leave Uppat yesterday, to go, I suppose, to Worsley, on his way to Trentham. Lord Harrowby is surprisingly well ; he has made Sandon a most agreeable and pretty place. I liked my visits very much, but am happy to find myself again at home.

They say one of the young Cawdors is to marry a Captain Balfour, and Lord Anson's daughter somebody. I did not know he had one old enough. They say they never have their children at home, and leave their boy all the holidays at school. There is a precedent for you. Adieu.

Most affectionately yours.

LETTER XVI.

La Spezia, November 9th, 1838.

We have been delighted with the journey from Genoa, though yesterday was unfortunately rainy, and we had not the distant views, which must be beautiful. We came along an excellent road near the sea (like the road to Helmsdale), through woods of orange trees, ilexes, olives, vines, and aloe hedges, which I thought were only to be seen in Sicily (we saw only one in flower), cypresses, and a palm or two, with myrtles and aromatic weeds. We slept last night at Chiaoari, where the light chairs now so common are made, and to-day we have crossed the Bracco Apennine, and descended after sunset to this beautiful bay. When we began dinner we heard very pretty music, and on looking out of the window saw a band of thirty-six sitting in the street under it with wind instruments, who played delightfully. Stafford is very anxious that they should be well paid. It was fine to-day, and we could walk up the hills and enjoy the summer weather and the whole thing.

LETTER XVII.

November 10th, 1838.

We have had another very pleasant day. At eight o'clock we all went in a boat from the pier at Spezia to see the wonder of a spring of fresh water rushing up from a very great depth in the sea, so strong that the boat could not be rowed within the circumference of some yards. We therefore could not judge of the freshness of the water; that about it was certainly very salt. The carriages were ready on our return at the pier, and we came on to Carrara, where we stopped to visit the workshops of several artists who are settled here on account of the neighbourhood to the quarries. We bought some vases and tables, and then walked to the quarries, up a magnificent valley. The quarries are very interesting, *matériel* and *locale* considered, and the situation would in itself be very striking. We did not return from our walk till after dark, and then came on one post to this beautiful place, with a very comfortable inn, by an excellent road in a starry night, through a balmy air.

LETTER XVIII.

Florence, November 14th, 1838.

I wrote from Lucca, whence we went to Pisa the day before yesterday, Monday. We had been to see the Baths of Lucca in the hills, and desired the children not to wait, but to proceed, to reach Pisa by daylight. We were rather later.

It rained hard most of Monday night, but yesterday morning the sun rose in a clear sky, and it felt like a summer day. Our windows looked on the Arno, and the streets were so soon dry that we walked in them as if there had been no rain, to the Campo Santo, Cathedral, etc., and in the afternoon drove to see some of the camels in the stone-pine wood on the grand-duke's farm in the neighbourhood. The sun was agreeable ; the Italian inns are generally much more so than those in France.

To-day we came here, and arrived before dark, and are comfortably lodged, with sunny rooms looking on the Arno. I have found a kind letter from Mr. Grenville,*

---

* The Right Hon. Thomas Grenville, Lord Grenville's brother, and collector of the celebrated Grenville Library, one of the glories of the British Museum.

giving directions of sculptors at Rome, which he got from
Lady Arundel.

We are not quite sure yet about our lodgings there, but
expect to hear from Mr. Gloag, who went to Leghorn to
embark on a steamboat for Rome.

We are very sorry for Lord J. Russell,* who seemed
very happy with her, and will now have the undivided care
of his, and probably of her, children on his hands.

                               Ever most affectionately.

Letter XIX.

When I wrote on arriving here, we had seen nothing
of the place. We have since that time been seeing everything, and have been very much and agreeably occupied
in so doing. The treasures of works of art are very great.
We have also much reason to be pleased with the civilities
of the court. They are very good people. The grand-
duke a quiet, stylish, not military gentleman of about
forty ; the grand-duchess, his second wife, Neapolitan,
good-natured looking, but without grace ; the dowager
grand-duchess (a Saxon) with much more manner ; and
a young arch-duchess of sixteen, rather overgrown in
height, but pleasing; and a little sister of the grand-
duke, deformed, and looking clever accordingly, as such
persons do.

There was great civility about our presentation last
week, which ended in our being privately received before

---

* Lady John Russell, whose death is referred to, had died after five years
of married life with her second husband, leaving by him two little daughters,
afterwards Lady Georgiana Peel and Lady Victoria Villiers, as well as several
children by her first husband, Lord Ribblesdale.

the ball, at which eighty other English were afterwards presented.

Harriet was made much of; danced with the grand-duke, who goes very conscientiously through all the steps.

We thought the whole affair very long, so much so that at the end, when he said there would be another ball this week, at which he hoped to see us, she and I expressed our fear of being obliged to leave Florence before it. However, since that the Carlisles have been longer on the road, and will not be here till to-morrow, and the poor maid whose arm was hurt will have to undergo another operation and then to be left here, so she wished to stay for those two reasons, and in the mean time an invitation, very long and beautifully written by the *grand maggior-domo*, came to dine at court (as) to-day, which is said to be a most unusual occurrence; and Madame de Gontaut (who is perhaps a little jealous of these honours to us, but probably not) has told me that it has been an affair of very great consultation and consideration, as court dinners are of extremely rare occurence. She had heard that they, after ascertaining if we would stay for it, were in a state about whom they should invite besides. They accordingly invited the Austrian minister as a family minister, and then were puzzled, as he is married, how to contrive that his wife should not be in the way of their civility to the *grande maîtresse* of the Queen of England. "Enfin," Madame de Gontaut said, "vous verrez comment cela se passera." We have now returned, very pleased with their kindness. Harriet was told, on entering, that she was to sit at dinner on the right of the grand-duke, between him and the grand-duchess, and I was told to sit between the dowager grand-duchess and the sister. The family all went in to dinner first, and Harriet and other ladies followed singly, then the Austrian and I together. The

R

Austrians and Lady Rendlesham, who has a house at Florence, were the only other *convives*, the dinner being for only twenty-two ; but in the great apartment I found the deformed grand-duchess, the sister, very well informed *about you* and Scotland, etc., and they were all as civil as possible.   We afterwards went to the Opera, for which Jerome, Prince de Montfort, who is living here with his daughter, who is a charming person, *ætat.* 18, had sent us his box.   The second court ball took place yesterday ; it was also rather long, but appeared less so than the first time.

They all seem much pleased with Harriet.

LETTER XX.

Rome, Friday, December 7th, 1838.

We arrived here prosperously on Tuesday, a day sooner than we had intended, having giving up the seeing Caprarola and Bagnaia from Viterbo, on account of the intelligence Vautini got of the *custode* of Caprarola having been taken up, as also fifty or sixty brigands, at the head of whom he was said to have been found out to have been.   I do not yet know what truth there may have been in it. But we thought it better to come on to Rome; and coming down the hill before the Ponte Molle, with Elizabeth in our carriage, that we might enjoy her first sight of Rome, we saw a large cavalcade ascending the road, which proved to be the Burlingtons, C. Percys, Sneyd, Lady Williams, and Miss Coutts Trotter, Lord Berkeley, and some others, which rather interfered with one's sentiment for Rome.   I found great changes in the Piazza del Popolo—new buildings and promenades and *trottoirs* in the streets, and more appearance of gaiety and crowd and shops than formerly.

Our house is rather far up, and hilly, past the Quirinal. The children are comfortably lodged. We passed most of Wednesday (after seeing the Burlingtons) in St. Peter's, where they and Sneyd also joined us; yesterday at the museum of the Vatican, and then dined quietly at the Burlingtons'. To-day we have been to the Lateran, Santa Maria Maggiore, and two or three other sights, and dined with the C. Percys, at a house you remember, the Margarita, in ascending to which from the Piazza di Spagna in the dark in our coach, we were somehow overturned— fortunately only ourselves in the carriage. Harriet had much presence of mind, and said, as we were going over, "What had I better do?" and did what was best—stayed back in her corner on the side on which we fell; and somehow I did not fall on her, and we escaped without any bad knock, so that when people came and put a chair into the coach to help her out, we walked on to the dinner. (This has happened on a Friday, as did the accident to the *fourgon* in the Alps, which will confirm Mr. Gloag in his opinion of its not being a lucky day.) There is great difficulty in finding a lodging for the Carlisles, who have arrived at Florence; and he seems to be pretty well again. I found a very melancholy letter from G. Harcourt here.

St. Peter's did not disappoint Harriet, and the Vatican exceeded her expectations; this I take from a letter she has written to Lady Carlisle.

I have been very glad to receive your letter of the 11th of November, after your Windsor visit, which I am glad that you have made, and that you are acquainted with the manner of the court there. Harriet has heard from the queen a good account of you. She said that you were occupied with your *potager*. If I can get any useful seeds for you I will. We have many flowers all round our house here. The Robert Grosvenors were gone to Naples before

we came. The Duke of Devonshire had gone to Albano
to shake off a cold. The children are all well. Lady
Burlington's boy,* whose health gave them uneasiness, is
looking very well, but is thought to require attention.

LETTER XXI.

Rome, December 14th, 1838.

I yesterday received your letter of the 30th, with some
account of a violent storm, which we have escaped. I hope
that the statue at Dunrobin may have escaped it. You
see that you must not believe newspaper accounts. Lady
M. Talbot † is perfectly well, and expecting her marriage
after, I believe, Easter. They had received accounts at
Florence of our having been robbed, and that Harriet was
carried into the mountains to ensure a ransom, and a Mr.
Frizellas (?), who used to live at Paris, took an opportunity
to inquire about it of Lady Carlisle and frightened her. I
am sorry to say that they are detained at Florence by his
having gout. We had taken rooms for them at an hotel,
and were expecting them when this account came yesterday. The Duke of Devonshire is here. Burlingtons,
Sneyd, all very well. The weather has not been fine till
to-day; we enjoyed it at the Coliseum, Baths of Titus,
Palace of Cæsar, etc. We are, of course, very busy seeing
sights. Some have improved of late years. Prince Borghese is replenishing the Casino at the Villa, which had been
stripped of its statues by the sale of them to the French,
with new discoveries made on different parts of his estates;
but the stone-pines are unfortunately wasting away. They
have planted several young ones to replace them.

* The late Lord Frederick Cavendish, M.P.
† Married Prince Philip Doria-Pamphilj.

We have not yet made acquaintance with the Borghese family, and are now likely to be prevented by a melancholy event in it ; their daughter, a handsome young Madame de M——, is very ill at Paris, and her death is expected.

Ever most affectionately.

LETTER XXII.

Rome, Christmas Day, 1838.

The bells of Santa Maria Maggiore are louder and more against sleep than the sound of those of Westhill, as one hears them at Westhill on Christmas Eve. In other respects our Christmas Eve was much like some English ; after a stormy night, when I thought the windows would be blown in, we found yesterday morning the ground covered with snow. We have been this morning attending the great ceremony at St. Peter's, with Lord and Lady Shrewsbury, in the balcony of Sta. Elena, the corresponding one to that of Santa Veronica, whence we had a very good view of the pope officiating and of all the ceremony, which I need not describe. Stafford and Mr. Jackson were in the opposite balcony. We have since been to vespers at Santa Maria Maggiore ; very good music. We are going to dine with the Torlonias, which it may seem not the day one would have chosen for so doing ; but we did choose it without considering, and afterwards found they had invited all our own friends here, to make it what they called a family dinner for us, including their own family too. I did not expect, before we came, to become so well acquainted as this implies, and one comes prejudiced against one's very rich banker, whose family have risen as they have. But besides being most obliging and attentive, they are an excellent family. The old man died, leaving most of the

fortune to his youngest son, the others extremely well
provided, but without much thought of his wife, the old
Duchess Torlonia. The sons were hurt at this neglect of
their mother, and told her that everything was hers; and
she is under the belief that it is accordingly all hers
(they also behaved admirably during the cholera at
Rome), and they all live on the best terms possible
together. The grand-duke arrived a few days ago, and
first appeared at a *soirée* for him at the Russian ambassador's, when we were all presented; I by Lieven, who
looks much older. On Saturday the Duke of Devonshire
and I received invitations to dine with the Cesarevitch on
Sunday, his first dinner. The Austrian and French ambassadors were the only other strangers, so we think that
England received a due attention in our persons, and we
have been invited before the envoys and others of the *corps
diplomatique*, which we also think very right.

LETTER XXIII.

Rome, January 2nd, 1839.

I do not know if you ever read Cardinal Pacca's
memoirs of the pope's being carried away from Rome to
Fontainebleau and Paris, and his own imprisonment at
Fontainebleau. He was the pope's minister at the time.
They are rather long and perhaps a little twaddling, but I
thought them very interesting, and it has made me and
the children, who have also been lately reading them, take
a great interest in the old cardinal; and Lord Clifford told
him so, and told me that the cardinal would have pleasure
in seeing me: and I accordingly paid him a visit, and
found him with sparkling eyes in his cabinet. I told him
what Pozzo di Borgo had said to me of his memoirs when

I mentioned them to him, " Mon cher duc reliez ce livre en cedre et or," which could not fail to please him. I think it was rather a strong recommendation of the book. I do not believe that the Buccleughs are coming here, as I hear they have taken a house, Lady Acton's, at Naples.

The Duke of Cambridge has been very kind in attending to my solicitation for Sir J. Macdonald, and is always very amiable and kind on all occasions. P. Lieven has been laid up for a week with a fever; better. Sir H. Taylor is better, but, I fear, in a precarious state.

I do not wish to imbue Trentham with the love of arts that poor Lord Cawdor used to wish to give the present Cawdor, after suffering himself for his fancies in that line. But he has already brought home some little bronzes he declares to be antique, and some allowed to be modern, to be stuck on bits of marble.

LETTER XXIV.

Rome, February 5th, 1839.

I was very sorry to learn by your letter of the 22nd that you had felt so unwell, and that the complaint had continued, though Sir H. Halford had hoped to have relieved you by his prescription. I have now received Mr. Loch's letter of the 24th, from which I trust that Dr. Chambers, whom I am glad that you consulted, has discovered the fault and the proper remedy. I am very sorry not to be with you while you have had these uncomfortable feelings. I hope that there has not been the same sort of pain which you have felt before, particularly once at Stafford House. Mr. Loch seems to have no doubt that Chambers has ascertained the cause of your complaint, and that his remedies will set all right, which I sincerely trust before this may have been effected.

The recovery of the Grosvenor child seems to have been very fortunate. She must have been well treated. Ours are all well, and some thinking much of the Carnival, which began yesterday.

Lady Burlington's lodging is in the Corso, so it will be a rendezvous for the family. Lord Carlisle will not be able to participate ; he is still suffering and confined to the house.   I believe this is not a good place for rheumatism I am very glad that the statues both at Dunrobin and Trentham have not suffered for that storm.   It must have been an unusual trial of the strength of these works, which will, I hope, long endure.*   One lives here among monuments.   We were all in the Catacombs last week, and in the *souterrains* of St. Peter's, and I have been in the vaults of the Capuchins, who live much among their dead, all which certainly brings one's mortality into one's thoughts, to which one must accustom one's self to be resigned, at all events.   We must all feel that we are very imperfect in many different ways, and place our reliance on a superior wisdom and trust to a merciful Creator. Our greatest happiness and comfort must be in our hope and faith in an Almighty Providence over us.   What you say about the blessings we in our family have and continue to enjoy we cannot be too thankful for.

Many loves to you from the children.   Harriet sends her kindest love, and we hope next post will bring another and a good letter from you.

Ever most affectionately.

This last letter of my father's to his mother reached

---

* This refers to the two colossal statues by Chantrey, of the first Duke of Sutherland, one at Dunrobin, the other at Trentham.

England after her death. I think the following extract from a letter written my father by his sister Charlotte, Lady Surrey, afterwards Duchess of Norfolk, will be appropriate here.

Extract of a Letter written on January 29, 1839, from Hamilton Place, after the death of the Duchess Countess, to my Father, by his sister, the Duchess of Norfolk.

"MY DEAR GEORGE,

"I open this to say something from myself which I am sure will be a very consolatory accompaniment to what you will hear from Mr. Loch, for I doubt not you will feel or think, as I do at this moment, that one should have done more if one had it to do again—I suppose everybody feels so when they lose a dear relation. She expressed but the other day to her maid (having herself from the beginning believed this to be her last illness) how fortunate she was and happy in her children being all good and affectionate ; and to Mr. Loch, at Dunrobin, how glad she felt it was to go to one after her who she was in every way so pleased with, and who would do it justice. She said to me the evening I arrived, before the wandering came on, that she thought she would not recover, that it was very well that it should be so, for she had had a long spell of life, and was perfectly ready to go ; that she left her family all in best possible condition, and all friends with no chance of their being otherwise. A more entirely easy, placid, contented, and serene last illness never can have been. The beauty of her character has shone conspicuously in it—never one word of complaint or impatience, but, as long as the power of speech remained,

always something considerate and kind to say to everybody that came near, and always the most gracious
pleasing way with regard to everything that was done
for her. . . . It is evident, as Lady Clarendon observed to
me, how beloved she is by her servants of every degree.
The queen has been very kind in sending to inquire."

Thus tranquilly passed away, at a ripe old age, beloved
by her family and esteemed by all who knew her,
Elizabeth, Duchess Countess of Sutherland, who, to quote
her old friend and countryman, James Loch (father of Sir
Henry Loch), was " one of the most remarkable persons of
her time."

THE END.

PRINTED BY WILLIAM CLOWES AND SONS, LIMITED, LONDON AND BECCLES.

www.ingramcontent.com/pod-product-compliance
Lightning Source LLC
Chambersburg PA
CBHW030356270326
41926CB00009B/1138